About Moss.

Moss is a literary journal of the Pacific Northwest. Founded in 2014, *Moss* is dedicated to exploring the intersection of place and creative expression while exposing the region's outstanding writers to a broad audience of readers, critics, and publishers.

Moss.

Volume Six.

M. A publication of Moss.
https://mosslit.com

Twitter: @mosslitmag
mosslit@gmail.com

Climate change is a global emergency.

Cover photo © 2017 Alex Davis-Lawrence
Interior photos courtesy of the US Forest Service / USDA

Printing by Bookmobile Printing Services
ISBN: 978-0-9969379-5-5

Printed in the United States of America
1 4 5 2 9 10 8 6 3 0

Contents.

Poetry

There's dynamism reflected in Indigenous languages. Often the dreamworld coalesces with so-called reality. The inanimate have souls—rocks, and trees, bodies of water. Everything has a narrative, has a story, and it's universally accepted that stories are medicine. That's poetry.

Tiffany Midge

Buckling of rails when trestle was destroyed by forest fire.
Pe Ell, Pacific Northwest Experiment Station, Washington. 1926.

Safe

Cari Luna

from The Death of Lorca

Anna's ex-husband used to say it's the things you never saw coming, the things you didn't even think to worry about, that'll take you out in the end. He said it when she got nervous before a transatlantic flight, or when she'd get that squirrelly panicked feeling in a big crowd where someone might start shooting. He said it when she got called back for a follow-up scan after a routine mammogram (which, yes, turned out to be fine). He said it when the pandemic first hit and she began to fear the air around her and the proximity of strangers and the thought that a single, careless breath could lead to complete collapse. The thing he would never hear, could never admit, was that every one of her fears was valid; that being dismissive of a danger is not, in itself, a protection against it.

But now? What's riding her now? She lies awake on her friend Lina's couch, eyes closed against the morning light streaming in through the window, and she pretends to be asleep as Lina and José bustle as quietly as possible between bedroom and bathroom, trying not to wake her as they go through their morning motions in the small apartment. Anna lies still and her heart pounds in her chest, her breath gone tight, and she acknowledges the fear coursing through her, charging her body electric, and acknowledges, too, that it has no name, no specific trigger. Just simple fear. Fear of whatever it is that's coming that she doesn't even know to expect.

Maybe it's the lack of sleep. She's too old to sleep on a couch like this. All night with the sofa buttons cutting into her back, and the streetlight nearly bright as day through the too-thin curtain. After five year of living in Portland, her brain has forgotten how to filter out the sounds of traffic. All night she reaches again and again for her phone to check for the email that never arrives, the text. Álvaro, gone silent on her again.

But no. Take a deep breath and start over. Eyes open.

Here she is on a Saturday morning in Manhattan, in the home of a dear friend. On the table across the room she can see the remains of last night's dinner: empty wine bottles and crusts of bread, crumpled cloth napkins. They had all been too tired, too sated, too warmly drunk to clean up before bed. They would do it in the morning, they'd promised each other. The dirty dishes would keep overnight, no harm in it. Anna lets her eyes fall closed again. She breathes. The fear goes slack and fades.

"It's on the dresser," Lina whispers, coming down the short hallway toward the living room. "I meant to show you last night."

And José whispers, "Yeah, okay, I'll call on Monday."

Nothing important, nothing they wouldn't say if they knew she was awake, but there's a softness in their voices, an unthinking intimacy to the simple business of shared lives, that makes her not want to open her eyes and intrude. And there's a pleasure, too, in bearing secret witness to this quiet space of their marriage, how they are for just each other.

But then she feels Lina draw close to the sofa and she does open her eyes, and Lina is there smiling at her. "You're awake," Lina says. "How did you sleep?"

I lay awake for hours thinking about the mom who lost her three kids when that Black church in Mississippi was firebombed last month, Anna wants to say. *I was thinking about how she collapsed at the funeral, how we all saw it online, how we played it over and over, consuming her grief.*

"Eh," Anna says. "My brain, you know? Always out to get me. How about you?"

And after that firebombing, the shooting at the Florida mosque. And then a shooting at a synagogue in Kansas. Then at a Black church in Texas. Then at an Islamic culture center in California. All in the space of a month.

She hoists herself up to make room for Lina, who sits, curling her legs beneath her. Down the hallway in the bathroom, the shower sputters on and José starts to sing in Spanish. Something about a dead dove, something about making a crown of flowers for it with his hands.

"I wish you would stay longer," Lina says.

Just three days, this visit to New York. Anna flew in from Portland for the panel about politically engaged fiction that she and Lina had been part of last night at the New York Public Library. It had been a good event, a quiet success, and tonight she'll fly home. But three days is a stupidly short amount of time to spend in the city where she was born. She should have allowed herself a full week here, at least. There hasn't been enough time to see even half the people she wanted to see. There's never enough time.

"They're doing *Bernarda Alba* at the Workshop in January," Anna says. "Maybe I'll come back for that."

"You and Lorca," Lina says, clucking her tongue.

"My dead boyfriend."

It's an old joke, but one that feels true, in its way. She was introduced to Federico García Lorca's poetry when she was fifteen, became fluent in Spanish solely (at first) to be able to read his work in the original language, and still feels a feverish sort of longing for him. That he died decades before she was born, and that he would have had no romantic interest in her, a woman, doesn't matter. It isn't a sexual longing; it's a soul longing. The longing for a sibling never met, or for some obscure part of her own self that can only be seen by his light. Now, at forty-six, she carries all the urgent tenderness for him that most at her age would feel, she supposes, for the memory of a first love.

Lina laughs and Anna remembers their video call of a few months ago when Anna confessed that in her next novel she would finally write about Lorca. Lina had paused and pursed her lips and said, not unkindly, "But don't you think the Lorca thing has already been very... done?"

"Not in English," Anna had said, but what she'd really meant was *Not by me*.

"So listen," Lina says now, coiling her damp hair into a neat bun. "José will be out of the shower in a minute and you can hop in and then we'll go out to get some breakfast."

Anna nods and Lina pats her knee and stands. "I'll make some coffee."

Anna checks her phone again. Nothing from Álvaro.

It's a little past 9am in New York. A little past 3pm in Spain.

She pictures Álvaro at his desk in the writing studio in his apartment in Madrid. She's never been there, because it's his wife's apartment, too, but he's sent her photos of the studio with its assorted animal skulls, its fetal pig in a jar, its collection of 1950s erotica. Late one night his time, early evening Anna's time in Portland, when his wife was out of town, he'd taken Anna on a video tour of the whole apartment, holding things up to the phone's camera for her to see: a taxidermy starling, a portrait of his mother painted on a walnut shell, a spoon stolen from Franco's palace. She'd shown him around her house, too, and he'd exclaimed over all of it—her overloaded bookcases, her old family photos, her collection of maps. She'd begun then to dare to imagine him in her home, sharing that space with her, but she knows it will never happen, likely not even for a visit. His next novel to be translated into English might bring him to the US, but not without his wife, Elena, along for the ride. Not that he even bothers to travel to the States to promote his books in translation. He doesn't need to do that bookstore song and dance anymore, like Anna does. He's Álvaro Cienfuegos, after all—Spain's bad boy literary darling now aged into an internationally beloved eternal-enfant-terrible cultural icon.

A cultural icon who's gone silent on her. No matter how many times she refreshes her inbox, she can't seem to make a response from him appear.

She's forty-six years old and in love like a teenager. Pathetic.

She hears Lina in the bathroom now with José, the shower turned off. She can make out the gentle play of their voices, but not the words. How good they are, how much sense they make, the way they've fit their lives together.

Somewhere out there in the city, Anna's ex-husband, Daniel, is either awake or still asleep, either alone or with someone else. She has no idea. When they divorced five years ago and she moved to Oregon, she let him go entirely. Daniel blamed the split on the quarantine, the endless months bleeding into more months. They were on top of each other and at each other's throats in their small Brooklyn apartment when the virus was still raging full force, but that wasn't really it. Anna had never been wholly herself when she was with him—she couldn't be; he made no room for it—and if anything the lockdown had held her even more in place.

That's how you do it, Álvaro. When a marriage isn't good for you, you walk away.

Lina's voice chases José's down the hall to their bedroom, the door latching closed behind them.

Anna brings her things to the bathroom, starts the shower, and steps in. Water sluices down the curve of a breast, the jut of a hip. Her white skin blooms up pink from the heat. Álvaro's mouth on that breast, his hand on that hip. How small she is beside him, beneath him. How soft and open, how humming with power. He touches her—has always touched her—as if she were a beautiful surprise.

"This Lorca novel," he'd said to her back in July, when they were last together in Madrid. "It's the best idea you've ever told me. You have to write it."

They'd been lying in bed, her cheek on his bare chest, and she'd felt his baritone rumble gently through her as he spoke. There had been pride in his voice. He was proud of her. To be proud of someone is to lay a certain claim on them—you can't be proud of what you don't consider, to some degree, your own.

She should remember his gentle claim on her good mind; she should remember his eyes and hands and mouth on her body; she should remember who and how she is each time she and Álvaro are finally returned to each other in the flesh, how they are for each other, skin to skin. She should hold fast to that, and not count the days that run into weeks each time he goes silent.

The morning light is doing that golden thing it does some days in New York, making everything go sharp-edged and true so you catch your breath at the hard beauty of it all. José peeled off straight away after breakfast and now it's just Anna and Lina walking together from Morningside Heights down into the Upper West Side of Anna's childhood. They walk just to walk, to be outside and in the sun and together.

They cut east to walk along Central Park West, the massive pre-war apartment buildings a cliff wall above them and across the broad street the park and its insistent trees, and the low stone wall border to hem in all the memories. With each block Anna sheds years, decades. Here, she's a sullen sixteen, walking as far behind her parents as they'll allow on a forced Sunday walk to the park from their apartment off of Riverside Drive. Here, she's eight or nine and racing her big brother, Todd, down this very block, from 93rd to 92nd, on the way back from a family lunch with Aunt Barbi.

Here, The Ardsley, Aunt Barbi's building with the same red awning as ever, the same heavy art-deco doors as ever. Beyond those brass doors, an ornate marble lobby ends in a massive mirror. When Anna and Todd were little they liked to pretend that they were visiting Aunt Barbi in a palace, and that the huge mirror was a portal to another world that one day, always some other day, they would step through.

As an adult, Anna would travel up here from Brooklyn to see Aunt Barbi at least once a month, which at the time seemed like plenty but in hindsight was not nearly enough. No amount of time is enough once someone you loved dearly is gone. You get greedy for it, looking back.

Aunt Barbi died of cancer at the peak of the first wave of the virus. She'd been sick for nine years, but when someone is sick for that long, with cycles of illness and remission, it's easy to forget where they were always headed, and so the loss felt sudden and cruel. The city was in lockdown by then, and Anna hadn't been able to visit her. And then just a week later, Todd had died of the virus. That loss truly sudden and unquestionably cruel. He was only forty-one, healthy and good. He was so good. Both of their deaths ghost through her now, their losses reverberating fresh and fierce, seven years later, on this known and surrendered territory. She swallows hard against the memories. Not now.

Anna nods to the doorman as they pass. He nods and smiles, then leans back in to his conversation with the building's private security guard. The guard, like all of the private security hired by the luxury buildings in the city these days, is kitted out in tactical gear and carries an assault rifle. The doorman, unarmored in his crisp white shirt, his black pants with the stripe down the leg, looks like a quaint, too-vulnerable throwback to another era.

These armed guards are all over Portland now, too. They've multiplied over the past year, since the shootings and bombings really picked up pace. Things change so quickly. Anna's eyes just skim right over the guards and the guns now, and she has to work to remind herself that it isn't normal, it shouldn't be normal.

When they're out of earshot Anna says to Lina, "My aunt used to live there."

"Fancy," Lina murmurs.

Anna bites back the justifications, the urge to say *Yeah, but the rest of the family never had that kind of money.* That doesn't matter now.

She didn't recognize the doorman; he must be new. But of course, it's been seven years since Anna last walked through those doors. She forgets how much time has passed and how much has changed. She forgets because she went away. She was one of the ones who ran. There's a shame in that, being one of the ones who left New York.

In the distance, from the south, a cracking sound like gunfire. Not just one or two, but a barrage, and then a pause, and then another run. Then another. Lina stops, reaching out to catch Anna by the shoulder. The guard outside of the building just ahead of them whispers into his radio, but doesn't leave his post. "Guns or fireworks?" Lina says.

"I mean—It would have to be a whole box of fireworks, that many pops in a row," Anna says.

"Or a whole box of guns," Lina says.

"Yeah but on the Upper West Side?" Anna says.

"Whatever it is, it's stopped."

It's a box of fireworks set off by accident by some kids, and hopefully no limbs lost. It's some kind of industrial machinery gone haywire. It's a movie set, just another goddamn movie set closing off an entire city block.

They start walking again, but slower now. Whatever's happened is somewhere ahead of them. Probably they should turn around, go back to Lina's apartment, and wait to read about it online. That would be the smart thing. But still. They don't even know for sure that there's anything to run from.

The sound of sirens now, but this is New York. There are always sirens.

"It stopped, anyway," Lina says again.

An armored police vehicle, cops in riot gear clinging to the sides like beetles, rolls slowly past them, headed north, away from whatever the gunshot sounds were. Used to be you'd only see those types of heavy police tanks at protests. Now they're as common on the street as taxis.

She shakes her head. No good down that path. "Hey," she says to Lina. "Tell me how your new novel is going."

Lina grimaces, but Anna knows not to read too much into that. Lina never says the work is going well, but the resulting books are often brilliant. "Eh. It's like unpacking an old trunk, this one. One dusty photograph after another and I'm running out of room to put them. I'm bored of it, really. Tell me about yours."

Three short, sharp cracks ring out. And a fourth. A fifth. Then silence.

"Those were gunshots for sure," Anna says.

Sirens and horns swell up behind them and two police cars go rushing by, lights flashing, followed by an ambulance and a firetruck. More flashing lights ahead in the distance, moving north toward them. The lights converge three blocks down at 83rd, some emergency vehicles turning in at the corner and others stopping right in the middle of Central Park West, blocking traffic in both directions. Blue police barricades are pulled from a van to close off the intersection completely. The sirens don't stop, more police cars, more ambulances. Cops step out into the street to redirect a stream of confused drivers.

"Should we turn around, or—?" Lina says.

"Let's maybe—Maybe we keep going another block and just see what we can see. It should be safe enough behind the police lines, right? Or they wouldn't be letting people stand there."

People crowd the barricades, craning necks, holding up phones to video whatever it is that's going on. Lina and Anna walk on, now part of a growing number of people streaming toward the scene. There's a sick familiarity to this, a particularly American curiosity in the face of presumed disaster. *You'd think we'd have learned by now that we are in no way immune*, Anna thinks. But everyone wants a firsthand glimpse. She's no different.

"So, your Lorca novel," Lina says, her voice straining toward normal.

"Right. Well," Anna says, "I've started working on it. I've got this scene with Lorca at a dinner party at Neruda's place in the Casa de las Flores. Lorca and Neruda, and Luis Cernuda is there, too. A table full of poets. And it's just before the civil war breaks out—which of course they don't yet know for sure is coming, but they're worried—"

Lina shades her eyes with her hand, trying to make out what's going on up ahead. "You know about Neruda, right? You know his reputation in

Chile is no longer—how do we say it? His reputation isn't so great these days. There was a daughter who had some kind of mental incapacitation and he abandoned her and the mother completely, but the big thing that turned people against him is that he raped a teenage servant when he was a diplomat in Sri Lanka."

"Shit."

"He even wrote about it in his autobiography like it was a funny little mistake he made. We Chileans—we're not so proud of him these days."

"Fucking Neruda," Anna says. "Damnit."

"But he should be in your novel," Lina says. "He was there, with Lorca. He should be there in your book. But when we write about the past, we have to explore it with what we understand now, in the present, no? The present interrogates the past."

At the corner of 83rd they step out into the street and weave through the crowd until they're up against the police barricade. Anna leans out over it to try to get a view down 83rd.

"Keep behind the line," a cop says, a hand drifting toward his baton.

"What happened?" she asks, nodding toward the mess of flashing lights.

He looks her over, decides she measures up, and says, "A shooting at the synagogue."

"Rodeph Shalom?" she says.

"Yeah, I don't know," he says, and moves on.

"I heard the whole thing, I swear to God," a woman is saying somewhere behind Anna. "I'm just over there on the sidewalk, okay, gonna meet my friend, and then all these shots pop off, right? And you can hear the screaming from here. Those poor people. And then the first cops come and bust on in and you hear more shots. I think they got the guys? I guess?"

"Rodeph Shalom," Anna says, a spike of fear hitting first at her jaw and then flooding through her. "That's where my family went to temple when I was a kid. It's just—" She gestures toward 83rd.

She feels Lina's arm around her shoulder, Lina's cheek pressed to her own. "Shh," Lina says. "Shh. You're okay," and Anna realizes that she's clinging to the barricade, that her body is shaking.

The synagogue is on the north side of the street, so Anna can't see it from where she stands. She only sees ambulances and police cars, and the brownstones across from the synagogue. The stoops of the brownstones are crowded with people. People weeping, holding each other, making frantic gestures as they speak to cops. People dressed up for Saturday morning services, sitting on dirty brownstone steps.

EMTs push a gurney out onto 83rd. There's someone in it, dark hair against a white pillow. The EMTs guide it down the street, past two ambulances and then out of view. There must be a line of ready ambulances, like an airport taxi stand. More ambulances line up along Central Park West, empty and waiting.

"Yeah they took 'em out," an older cop is saying to the one Anna talked to. "Three of them. All clear now."

"Lina," Anna gasps. Lina guides her away from the barricade, through the crowd and out into the open, the middle of shut-down Central Park West. She takes a deep, shuddering breath, and another and another.

Sitting with her parents while the rabbi droned on, her dress stiff and itchy, wishing she was old enough to sit in the back of the sanctuary with Todd and the other big kids, wishing the service would just be over and they could go finally go home. And then a gunman—or gunmen...

Three of them. All clear now.

An older woman stumbles against Anna, who catches the woman's elbow to steady her.

The woman is weeping, and she looks at Anna and says, "I should have been there. I'm there every Saturday, but today I didn't..."

"Oh!" Anna says, clapping a hand over her mouth. This woman, her kind face. Her living face. The sanctuary would have been full of living faces. A hundred or more.

"I'm so glad you're safe," Lina says.

"Safe," the woman says. She could be Anna's mother. She could be any Jew at all, devastated but unsurprised.

"Are you okay?" Lina asks. "Do you want us to see you home, or...?"

The woman shakes her head, squeezes Lina's hand, and says, "You take good care of your friend here." She cups Anna's cheek with a warm papery hand, and says to Lina, "This is a bad day for the Jews. You take care of this one."

Anna kneels beside Lina's coffee table, the contents of her small suitcase spread out around her on the floor, her body angled away from the TV screen. José has tuned in to a news channel, even as he's scrolling through the same news on his phone.

"I thought you already packed," Lina says, stepping over a stack of clothes to set a tray of coffee mugs onto the table. She hands a mug to José and settles down next to him on the couch.

"I just want to make sure I have everything," Anna says. She shakes out a rolled t-shirt, rerolls it, and wedges it into a corner of the suitcase. She can feel Lina watching her, waiting for her to speak. Lina's concern falls thick over her, and she shrinks beneath it, folding closed around the pain.

"Authorities are already calling this morning's shooting at the Rodeph Shalom Synagogue in Manhattan an act of domestic terrorism," the newscaster says. "A representative for the FBI says the shooters have been linked to a known white nationalist militia based in rural Pennsylvania. A manifesto—"

"Of course, there's a manifesto," José says.

Lina says, "There's always a manifesto."

"My grandfather told me once that by the time our civil war started in Spain, there were as many manifestos circulating as there were guns," he says.

Anna takes the rolled-up t-shirt back out and stuffs it inside one of the dress boots she wore for the event at the library last night, then nestles both boots into the bottom of the suitcase. Yesterday, walking with Lina into the New York Public Library past those stately lions, Anna had felt strong. She had been excited to have been invited there, to belong there. There's a validation in events like those that you aren't supposed to admit to needing or wanting, but who doesn't want to be one of the ones up on the stage being asked questions on important topics because they've been identified as a person who Knows Things, who should be listened to. A thinker. Who doesn't want to be respected as a thinker? And there were those library lions of her NYC childhood to welcome her. A pleasure, that panel.

And then today. And now this.

"The three shooters," the newscaster says, "all killed when police arrived on the scene, are reported to have been private security guards hired by the congregation in response to the spate of recent attacks."

"Are they saying how many dead yet?" Anna says.

"No, querida," Lina says. "I think all I've heard so far is—"

"Dozens," José says. "At the beginning they just said dozens."

Murdered by the people they'd paid to keep them safe.

Anna shoves the rest of her clothes blindly into the bag and zips it shut.

"Hey, come sit next to me and drink your coffee," Lina says.

Anna sits and takes up the mug. She sips the coffee. She focuses on the good coconut scent of Lina's shampoo. She follows her breathing. This crisis is not new. This fear is not new.

The news segment about the synagogue shooting ends and the stories roll on: an effigy of the current president, a Democrat, was burned at the West Virginia state fair, the match lit by the Republican governor. A twenty-year-old Pakistani food-delivery driver was dragged from his car at a red light in Boston, and hasn't been found. A small town in Idaho has announced its intention to secede from the Union, and is angry that the federal government hasn't yet sent officers to try to stop them.

"They're not taking us serious," their representative tells the reporter. "But we're serious. Dead serious. We do not recognize the illegitimate government occupying the White House."

"Can they do that?" Lina asks.

"I mean, they can try," Anna says. "It usually ends in a shoot-out with the feds." Which this group in Idaho knows even better than she does. Maybe that's what they're hoping for: To make enough sparks to start a fire.

This America of deep, angry divides—of generations-long blood feud and resentment—terrifies her. Maybe every generation has worried over that divide, but these days it feels like the country has reached a true breaking point.

A Black church firebombed in Mississippi.

A shooting at a Florida mosque.

A shooting at a synagogue in Kansas.

A shooting at a Black church in Texas.

A shooting at an Islamic culture center in California.

And before that: A Mexican-American family executed in their own home by a vigilante border patrol in Arizona. And before that: Subway bombs that failed to go off here in New York. And before that: Bombs that did go off on a commuter train in Chicago.

And today. The shooting today.

Anna leans back against the couch and closes her eyes. Lina takes her hand and holds it, and they sit like that, quiet, as the newscast drones on.

At her gate at the airport, with a half hour until boarding, Anna sits with a habitual book open on her lap even though she's too distracted to read. She's got a cup of coffee on the floor next to her feet, but her stomach is already churning with nerves. The high ceilings of the concourse amplify the voices of the crowds, the echoes, the harsh light and hard edges. Everything feels sharp and dangerous. Bad things happen in crowded spaces like this. Bad things happen all the time.

There'd been a knot of guys ahead of her in the security line, four of them talking loud in flat midwestern accents. They wore the red hats of the deposed regime, and American flag patches on their matching black duffel bags. They were young and white, taking up space. One of them flashed a swastika tattoo on the back of a calf as he bent to take off his shoes—military-style boots, the tan desert-war kind, not the black boots of the Left. Military-style haircuts when they had to take the hats off to go through the body scanner. It's hard to tell if guys like those are immediately dangerous or if they just want to look like they are. Either way, they made Anna nervous.

Fifty-seven dead in today's shooting, twenty more injured.

Anna tried to scroll through the photos of the victims in the *Times*. She didn't recognize most of the faces—even before she left New York she hadn't been to temple for years and years—but then there were Bev and Larry Schwartz; there was George Klein; there was old Mrs. Messinger. These had been the grownups when she was a kid. She stopped scrolling after Mrs. Messinger. It was just too much.

Later, when she's home alone, she'll sit down and take her time with it, find some way to bring respect to the digitized faces.

But not here, sitting in an airport, swiping through the photos with her thumb like they're just so much *content*.

Any shooting is a tragedy. Of course. Of course. But always at a certain remove, always in the abstract. A horrifying story on the news. Today... this is how it feels when it could have been you. Jews were targeted this morning. Jews have been targeted for centuries. It's okay for Anna to admit that she, too, feels targeted right now. Here she is, with her Jewish name, her Jewish face.

These white nationalist groups have been threatening big trouble for decades. They've been threatening for so long that Anna, like most who've been paying attention, never really thought they would or could make good on it. But the attacks just keep piling up.

She wasn't going to write to Álvaro again until he responded to the email she sent six days ago, but...

She thumbs a quick note into her phone.

> Hey you. Greetings from JFK airport. I'm safe and sound, whatever that means these days. I did that event at the big public ibrary—the fancy one with the lion statues out front—with Lina Meruane last night, and it went well. You would have liked it, I think.
>
> Things are heating up here in the States, with the militias and all that crap we talked about the other week. You probably saw the news about the shooting today. That was my old neighborhood where I grew up. My family's old synagogue. Not that I've been there in years. Not that I've been to any synagogue in years. But still.
>
> Things feel precarious in a new way. I don't like it.
>
> (I'm on sabbatical for the whole school year, remember... Maybe I'll come visit you a little earlier than we planned. Ha!)
>
> Bueno...I'm here at the gate for the next little bit, if you feel like talking.
>
> Besos y besos, tesoro

She hits "Send," knowing he probably won't write back before she boards the plane. Knowing he might not reply for days.

Álvaro told her that he loved her once, in a text message the day after their last night together, back in July in Madrid, when he was still drunk, maybe, on the pleasures of their stolen time in her rented bed. He took that "I love you" back three days later as a slip, a mistake. Love isn't something the mistress of a married man gets to insist on.

Twenty-six years ago, when Anna was studying in Madrid for her junior year in college, a Spanish friend dragged her to a reading, the launch of the latest book by acclaimed novelist Álvaro Cienfuegos. Though she hadn't yet read any of his books, Anna had ideas of how Álvaro would be. She was wary of writers who were treated—and were rumored to behave—like rock stars. But at the event he'd sat on a stool at the back of the bookstore and read a passage that shocked her with its candor and humor, with its intelligence and near magical ability to draw the listener in and make them complicit. She'd been utterly won over. Her voice shook when she spoke to him as he signed a copy of the book for her; her palms went sweaty when his blue eyes met hers. And then he'd done the unthinkable and asked her to have a drink with him afterward. She was in his bed only a few hours later (he was between marriages at the time) and she stayed there—leaving only to go to class—for two weeks.

And then the semester ended and she'd had to fly home. There had been letters for a while, and a few expensive phone calls, and then he'd faded away and she'd let him go. He belonged to her life in Madrid, and she was back home in New York. He was a lovely ghost. She'd held fast to his memory for a while, and then had let him sink into history.

Their first night together, after they'd fucked, lying together all sweetly spent, lacing fingers like you do when everything is new and you're dazed by each other, they'd traded life stories. He, the Spanish atheist Catholic that he was, had been fascinated—almost turned on—to learn that he'd bedded a Jew. "Jewish Princess," he'd said proudly. (He'd learned the term from a Frank Zappa song, and he was so pleased with himself that she hadn't had the heart to explain that it was an insult.)

"No," she'd said. "I'm not the princess. I'm the dragon."

In June of last year Anna had gone to the Feria del Libro in Madrid to promote the Spanish edition of her fourth novel, and she'd seen Álvaro from across the room at a reception for authors. He was older, she was older, but there they were. Her stomach roiling with nerves, she'd gone up to him prepared to say, "Hi. I'm Anna Berman. We knew each other for a little while twenty-something years ago," but even as she opened her mouth to speak he looked at her with those same blue eyes and said, "Hello, Dragon."

Because he's married now, it was Anna's hotel bed they fell into that time, and he would leave it just before dawn to slink back home each of the five nights they had together, blaming book festival commitments for his absences. Five nights together in Madrid, and then countless emails and texts and secret phone calls after she'd flown home. She'd gone back to Spain in March, over spring break, to do research for the Lorca novel (and to be with him), and he'd managed three full days and nights away from his wife in Madrid, and two more in Granada. And then she'd gone back again in July, and they'd had four sweet, stolen nights.

And then that "I love you" that he rescinded three days later.

What happened was that she'd texted "Trust your dragon" in response to something they were joking around about, and he'd replied, "I love my Dragon."

"Oh!" she'd typed. "Oh, I love you, too!"

Then he'd abruptly had to sign off—which wasn't unusual. Then two days of silence, then when they were texting again she said she loved him and he said, "I like you very much. No digamos amor."

"But you said you loved me," she'd said, feeling pathetic and childish as she typed it, such a sad little protest.

"Yes," he'd said. "I used that word."

But he hadn't meant it. It had been a slip. They'd been texting mostly in English, and love doesn't always mean "amar" or even "querer." It had been a question of translation, he said. What she'd heard as his love for her had fallen into that slippery space between the two languages. He claimed that he had meant to say "me encantas"—you enchant me—and she had heard instead what she wanted to hear: That she was loved. Which was—she still insists—what he actually said. He said love. He said it. *He used that word.* But no.

That was two months ago, and since then the space between emails and texts has grown. He's been less available, and signs off in the middle of conversations—particularly if she gets too sentimental. He doesn't want to sext much at all, when before they would fuck via text for hours, sometimes until well after sunrise in Spain. Now it's been six days since she's heard from him. He's ignored two emails, not including the one she just sent, and several texts. He's distancing himself. He'll say he isn't, but he is.

Her phone rings. Not Álvaro. Her mother.

"Mom," Anna says. Gunshots. Dark hair against white sheets on the gurney. The long line of ambulances, waiting.

"Oh, baby." Her mother is crying. Nothing rips such a precise hole in Anna as the sound of her mother crying. "You're okay? You're still in New York?"

"I'm okay, Mom. I'm at the airport." And Anna, who'd been holding tears back for most of the day, is crying, too.

"Oh thank God." In the background, she hears her father saying, "She's okay?"

"Mom, I'm okay, but listen. Mom, I was there right after. I was just a few blocks away from the synagogue when—And I walked there to see what—I didn't know—And oh, Mom—"

"Thank God you're okay."

"And Bev Schwartz, Mom. And Larry. And Mrs. Messinger and—"

"I know, baby."

And that other woman, the one who was supposed to have been at Saturday services, but who stayed home. And all of the others who hadn't stayed home, who were there and who died, or had been shot and lived but would maybe die still, and all of the others who hadn't been shot, but will have to live out the rest of their lives with the stain of what they survived, with the absolute knowledge that what their grandmothers had always whispered was true—that we aren't safe in this world, that we have never been safe in this world.

She swallows hard, tries to force back the tears. She shouldn't cry in public like this. Ceding even a few inches of ground to those assholes, letting her self-control slip, is intolerable. Her tears would please them. They want her scared. They want her sad and broken.

After today, Anna understands the urge to kill all of your enemies. It's a survival impulse. She wants to kill them right now—all the racist, fascist, anti-Semitic assholes—before they can kill her and the people she loves. She wants them dead because they scare her.

Except she couldn't kill anyone. A gun in her hand right now, and a militia man with a gun in front of her? She couldn't, and she knows it. But the militia man probably could. And that difference, the gulf between Us and Them, is where terror is born.

My body is the house I haunt

Kaitlyn Airy

after Ocean Vuong

In the mouth of summer, where everything is sweet
                I was a girl, living

in my mother's house. From linen I wrung, not
                water, but blood, bright

as fresh birth, heavy as wet
                clouds. Even my grandmother

crawled out of her wedding day, begging
                forgiveness. We laid in the prairie, the sun

having its way. What arrived some months later
                rattled a tin cup. For in the mouth of summer

where everything is sweet, I was a gorgeous
                mistake. At times I would paint

the most striking color; alizarin
crimson, sunshine & avarice.

While bathing in exile on the shores
of the Salish sea they say I drove him mad

with song. Usually, I don't feel
powerful. I laughed until

I didn't. He chased me so far even the gods
took notice. This time, I became a laurel. There

are many women. There are many
trees. Sometimes we take root. Sometimes we

bloom. We sing to bring our ghosts

home.

Tiffany Midge in conversation with Amy Wilson

Spring 2021 · Digital Exchange

Tiffany Midge is a citizen of the Standing Rock Sioux nation, and a poet and writer of creative nonfiction, and fiction. Her work has appeared in *McSweeney's*, *Indian Country Today*, *Massachusetts Review*, *Hunger Mountain*, *Waxwing*, *GAY Magazine*, *YES! Magazine*, and more. Her poetry collection The Woman Who Married a Bear (University of New Mexico Press) received the Kenyon Review Earthworks Indigenous Poetry Prize, and her essay collection *Bury My Heart at Chuck E. Cheese's* (Bison Books) was a finalist for a Washington State Book Award. Midge is the recipient of a Pushcart Prize, a Simons Public Humanities Fellowship, and an Eliza So Fellowship. Her book of poetry, *Horns*, is forthcoming from Spokane-based Scablands Press. Midge's essay "The Jimmy Report" originally appeared in *Moss* Volume Two in summer 2016. A former poet laureate of Moscow, ID, Midge aspires to be the poet-in-residence at Seattle's Space Needle.

Amy Wilson, a poet and organizer from Oregon who serves on the volunteer leadership team of *Moss*, interviewed Midge by digital exchange.

Wilson

Hi Tiffany! Thank you for doing this interview with Moss. What is your personal connection to the Pacific Northwest? In what ways (if any) does the culture of the Pacific Northwest influence your writing?

Midge

I was born in Auburn, Washington, south of Seattle. My parents relocated from eastern Montana for employment opportunities, and my paternal (white) grandparents lived in Auburn. They formerly lived in eastern Montana also. I write about my life and experiences growing up in Washington. Before we moved to Kirkland, the eastside suburb of Seattle, we lived in Snoqualmie Valley, where my Dad taught in public schools. You mention culture, and there was a stark contrast of cultures from rural, dairyland and woods, to denser population, commerce, and suburbia. Those years in Snoqualmie Valley seem much more vivid and strange. The environment and the people held a quality of sureality that I could best describe as *Twin Peaks*. But there were idyllic, *Mayberry R.F.D.* / Frank Capra aspects to growing up there, also. There were no limits as to where I could explore, or how long I could be outside. I spent all my time in the woods, at the river banks, in pastures, and roaming through town, in and out of people's houses. And because my dad taught at the high school, we were often hanging out at his high school events and games. I've written about it throughout the years, and surprise myself sometimes because I'm still writing about it. Those young years of mine. Jesus. White people who live in the woods. Yeah. But my homelife was weird, and definitely offbeat, too.

Wilson

It is so funny to hear you bring up *Twin Peaks* as an accurate depiction of the environment and people you encountered in the Snoqualmie Valley. That show really has become a defining text of the Northwest! It's also interesting to hear you reference *Mayberry R.F.D.* / Frank Capra and this vision of Americana wholesomeness in the context of the Pacific Northwest. My own dad who lived in Vancouver, Washington as a child in the 1950s and 60s has said the same thing. It seems to me in many ways these are facets of the same thing about the Northwest—the strange and surreal exists side by side with the wholesome and straightforward. I see that a lot in one of my personal favorite writers of the Northwest, Ken Kesey. Aside from Twin Peaks, what other texts say "Northwest" to you? Do you have favorite writers or artists of the Northwest, either those working right now or from our history?

Midge

That's a fun question. And it's great to know you're a fan of Kesey, I don't hear younger generations bring up his work very often. He's featured in one of my flash pieces, "The Woman Who Married a Bear." Which is really a vignette that's part of a larger piece about kismet and synchronicity. I also mention his work, *One Flew Over the Cuckoo's Nest* in another vignette from *Bury My Heart at Chuck E. Cheese's*, about my father (who is white) playing the role of Chief Bromden in a theater production. I often approach novels with Native characters written by non-Native authors with some wariness, but *One Flew Over the Cuckoo's Nest* is kind of "grandfathered in"—much like David Seals's *Powwow Highway*, Tom Spanbauer's *The Man Who Fell in Love with the Moon*, or W.P. Kinsella's *The Fencepost Chronicles*. It's hard to scrutinize those books, but then again, I haven't read them in twenty years or more, either.

Northwest writers who've made an impact on my literary soul... in the early days, late 80s, early nineties, I took poetry classes, extended ed. classes offered at UW, from Nelson Bently, and Beth Bently. They were great. Nelson was a co-founder of *Poetry Northwest* and *The Seattle Review*, and his Friday night Castilia Reading Series might still be going on. He is the only poet I know, to this day, who used call and response audience participation in his poetry readings. And he was a finessed speaker of Old English. He always invited folks out for drinks at the Blue Moon Tavern after the readings.

I lucked into taking a day long workshop with William Stafford that made a big impression on me. He was very kind and supportive of some of my earliest efforts at writing poems. I took creative writing classes at Seattle Central Community College from J.T. Stewart, and edited on *The Ark*. Her classes were very lively and mutually supportive. I got a lot out of them, she's a wonderful poet and teacher. I experienced some real coming-of-age chapters through the friendships I made with that group of students. Babies were conceived and born. Not my own, but fellow students who I became close with. I came close to making babies with someone from the class, though. Or would have liked to.

I spent many Sunday nights with the poets from Red Sky Poetry Theater, a core group who were anarchists, activists, and proletariat poets. It was a very vibrant and exhilarating scene. I read my first poems at a Red Sky open mic, after spending months and maybe years, screwing up my courage to present a poem. I don't remember ever being that nervous— shaking, and my knees literally knocking together. I only mention that by way of offering encouragement to writers starting out. It's daunting, it still is!

Eventually, my poems made it into the *Raven Chronicles*, and I felt like I'd arrived. One of the editors, Phoebe Bosche, was active with Red Sky, and along with folks like Kathleen Alcalá and Philip Red Eagle, they founded and produced this art and literature magazine centered upon multiculturalism with a strong emphasis on Native American art and literature. I felt a strong sense of belonging with Raven Chronicles, an authentic sense of community, and I continued to publish my work with the magazine, and to work on various projects and events with them, up until the present.

I enjoyed a lot of planning meetings for Native writing conferences and events in the Seattle area, and a lot of get-togethers, lots of readings, with the afore-mentioned Phil Red Eagle, along with Gladys Cardiff, and Gail Trembley, Duane Niatum, and several others. It was a nurturing environment for a young writer, very mutually supportive. I was always meeting new people, Native artists and writers, going out and socializing, there was always a literary event to attend, a soiree or after-party. I loved that.

My favorite books were and remain to be by Raymond Carver, Tom Robbins. Good lord! Katherine Dunn! Who could leave *Geek Love* out of such a list. Ursula K. Le Guin, of course. I've always been a big fan of Shawn Wong's *American Knees*. Also, Kathleen Alcalá, Jess Walters, Sharma Shields, Eden Robinson, Donna Miscolta, Anita Endrezze. And essayists Elissa Washuta, Danielle Geller who lives in Victoria now, Deborah Miranda, and Sasha LaPointe. Poets include our new Washington State poet laureate Rena Priest, Laura Da', Cedar Sigo, and Michael Wasson.

Wilson

Your recent book, *Bury My Heart at Chuck E. Cheese's*, is positioned as a humorous collection of essays and indeed, it is very funny. ("Reel Indians Don't Eat Quiche: The Fight for Authentic Roles in Hollywood" and "Jame Gumb, Hero and Pioneer of the Fat-Positivity Movement" were personal favorites of mine!) Yet there are many pieces and moments in the book that deal with serious topics, from personal grief and challenging familial relationships to Indigenous genocide and the rise of Trumpism in the US. Why use humor to frame these topics? What is your perspective on the relationship of humor in writing to the other types of emotions writing might inspire?

Midge

It's organic, for the most part. And isn't comedy and tragedy, the sacred and the profane, between laughing and crying, all a part of the same spectrum? Jokes and humor are my go-to because that's how the world presents itself to me. I suppose I look for the amusing, irreverent details to keep myself from going crazy. Or from being bored to death by the onslaught of our news cycle. It's a form of survival. Responding with satire, and with cynicism makes sense out of things that make no sense. And if I can't make sense out of whatever thing, I can at least use it as material, make something out of the thing, transcend it to the level of art. Just today I saw a meme with an explanation of how heyokas exist(ed) within D/N/Lakota society, and their function. The idea that a person who got too arrogant or full of themselves would be a target of teasing and ridicule from a heyoka. Maybe those types are all too common by today's standards, like Trump, for instance. And it is pretty obvious that the D/N/Lakota metric of a heyoka would succinctly apply. And that kind of teasing is a huge part of the entertainment/political humor industry.

Wilson

You are also a poet (a poet laureate of Moscow, Idaho, in fact!). Reading the essays in *Bury My Heart at Chuck E. Cheese's*, I saw so much poetry in the structure of your work (especially in Parts I and II) and in your use of imagery. Can you tell me a little bit about your philosophy of poetry? What makes something a poem?

Midge

I'm formerly a poet laureate of Moscow, Idaho, with aspirations to be distinguished poet laureate of Seattle's Space Needle. Which isn't an actual thing, yet, but should be. Poetry is baked into the fritatta of everyday life—or lasagna, apple pie, tuna casserole, what have you. It transcends beyond simply language and words. It is a lifestyle brand. A spiritual contract (hopefully) one makes with the world. It's an agreement with the cosmos to see "into" and "outside" of whatever boring or literal thing is being presented. I think poets are seers, visionaries, and soothsayers. Poetry should be as revered as religion and spiritual practices in this country, there should be poetry cathedrals and poetry churches and poetry ministries. Indigenous peoples are of this understanding. Indigenous peoples embody poetics within their everyday, traditionally. There's dynamism reflected in Indigenous languages. Often the dreamworld coalesces with so-called reality. The inanimate have souls—rocks, and trees, bodies of water. Everything has a narrative, has a story, and it's universally accepted that stories are medicine. That's poetry.

Wilson

Please excuse me while I take a quick break from this interview to get "poetry is baked into the frittata of everyday life" tattooed somewhere on my body... as a poet myself, I truly appreciate this perspective on poetry. It reminds me of the Worker Writers School organized by Mark Nowak, author of *Social Poetics*. His philosophy is also very much about seeing poetics in the everyday, whether that be on a factory floor, during a home health aide's meal break, or in a cab driver's cab. Yet poetry is often rarefied and institutionalized in this country, or assumed to be a pursuit of the wealthy and idle. Maybe that's an aspect of the white supremacy and settler-colonialism this state is founded on, to attempt to strip land and people of their poetics. I certainly feel that capitalism is a series of attempts to strip working peoples' lives of their poetry. What do you think would shift if we were able to institute what you suggest, to have "poetry cathedrals and poetry churches and poetry ministries" that were truly open to all?

Midge

We'd have a lot more poets. What if every corporate business and every institution had a poet in residence? Does Microsoft have a poet in residence? Does Boeing? And a poet for every county, town, and governmental department. Every library and bus station and sporting arena? Hospital poets. Can you imagine? It'd be like a speculative novel. The shift would be that poets wouldn't be hired just for presidential inaugurations. And that poets might edge out the National Anthem singers at baseball games.

Maybe that's one of the attractions of going to church—to sit with liturgy, devotionals, and scripture, to be with language and commune with it. There are similarities between a sermon and a poetry recitation, with regards to rhythms and inflections and speech patterns. Some poets can punch you in the gut, just as some pastors can bring people to their knees. Both experiences can be cathartic, emotional, a high. I spent a lot of time in bars and coffee houses for poetry open mics. And I've also sat in and experienced Catholic charismatic revivals, and Pentacostol ministers speaking in tongues. I've never seen anyone pass out and convulse at a poetry open mic, but I knew a woman who often seemed orgasmic.

Thinking about your comment about society, or our robot overlords, stripping people of their "poetics," makes me think of Indigenous songs. Honor songs. The idea that there is a song individually or collectively, created for all kinds of occasions. It's like a kind of prayer, or acknowledgement. And the idea that every being, be it animal, rock, tree or river has its own song, too. And we know that science has proved that to be true—that there are frequencies, and energies connected to every thing. There are a lot of analogies for what a poem is, and could be. But in this context, it could be the voice (or song) of one's soul.

Wilson

Many of the essays, especially in the latter half of the book, address the atmosphere in the US around the time of Trump's election and the days immediately after. Reading them in 2021, I was struck with memories of those difficult days and the feeling of fear and dread that pervaded many of our lives. What was your experience as a writer and artist in the Trump years? What (if any) sources of hope were you able to draw on? Do you think these years have affected your work now and if so, how?

Oh, for sure, there was a tremendous amount of "influence" on my life as a writer. And those sections in my book—and several others in earlier sections, also—are manifestations (infestations?) of that. There's no way around it, I mean, there's a cartoon of Trump on the book's cover! Leading up to the election, and the months following, I had been publishing all of the pieces as a column for *Indian Country Today*, so ICT is hugely responsible for *Bury My Heart at Chuck E. Cheese's* being a book. Writing (and publishing) the columns was a hope-generating exercise. And this is true of any humorist or comedian. The country tunes into Stephen Colbert or Trevor Noah to be lifted, to transcend the despair and hopelessness of the news cycle. And in the simplest way possible, really, by just laughing. Laughing at one's enemy is the ultimate defense, it's akin to counting coup. Or as I mentioned earlier, a heyoka's target for diffusing tension, healing, and reinstating harmony.

Insofar as the those years affecting my present work, it is likely that because of social movements, such as #WritersResist, and Black Lives Matter, along with #OwnVoices and #PublishingPaidMe, BIPOC artists are given more visibility, and more opportunities, and those social reforms have resulted in more doors being opened. A lot more doors. And I look forward to seeing the impact of those reforms.

The day after the 2016 election I posted these thoughts to my socials:

> Cinema attendance was at an all-time high during WWII. I think of this as I wake to the realization that we're living in a real time Dystopian YA novel, or just on the brink of it. And if the entertainment industry thrived in our depressed and harrowing era of war, back when the actual Hitler rose to power, it occurs to me that artists and creators are critically necessary now more than ever. Not just for escape and entertainment though, but for imagining better worlds, for instilling hope, beauty, ushering thoughtfulness and analysis.

So great to know about *Indian Country Today* and how their publishing your columns led to what became your book. You talk about social reforms in publishing and how these have led in the past few years to greater access and visibility for BIPOC writers, but it seems there's still a long way to go before there is full equity for workers and artists in the publishing industry. Part of the mission for us at Moss is to build up alternative platforms and networks to counter what we see as inequities (in our case, regional ones) in the way the culture industry is structured. You could even call us "counter-cultural" ;-)

Your essay for Moss, "The Jimmy Report," also appears in *Bury My Heart at Chuck E. Cheese's*. One of the reasons I love that piece is its honest depiction of culture in a small-town environment of Bellingham—the quirky thrift shop, the sidewalk busker, the local tavern, the ways that sad and un-pretty realities can mix with moments of transcendence and joy. There's also a wonderful piece in *Bury My Heart* about your experiences in a community theater growing up. Could you speak a little bit to the ways that culture shows up in these "unexpected" places, places that tend to be ignored by the wider world but are very alive to the people who live and experience within them?

Midge

It could be my age, and how different the social climate is, it could be the region I've lived in since 2005, going from Seattle to Idaho, there's a lot of contrast there, but it felt like I was more immersed in grass roots, working class theater/literary artists, dance-around-the-fire, removed from academia careerism, kinds of "culture" when I lived in Seattle. Maybe it's just nostalgia? Or maybe I've just become more reclusive. Obviously, living in a small town, there aren't as many artistic niches. Maybe I haven't discovered any weird enough people? Maybe I should move to Portland? It makes sense. I relocated to Idaho to pursue a degree, and although I loved the process, I loved learning, I didn't really find the same kind of "culture" in academia. Does that sound awful? Maybe not the "culture" I was used to? Maybe academia is a nice living, and a comfortable environment, but is also a little antiseptic? One hears about academia being antithetical to art, or in this case, poetry and writing. And so often one reads about the negatives of the MFA industry. I don't know. Having gone to two community colleges, and two different 4-year universities, I think I can say that I felt exceedingly more "at home," and "in the stream of life" insofar as the arts—writing, theater—while attending community college, than I did at larger universities. A lot of that might be due to community college having more non-traditional students, and more people with jobs and families, etc… community colleges are more of a way station to someplace else, and that attracts different kinds of people, with different wants and needs. Easily, one could make a case for a non-academic approach in pursuit of a literary life. We don't have the same expectations for the workaday as we would for a graduate degree program, and perhaps it allows for more freedom, takes away the pressure, and ultimately creates more spontaneous, organic events and situations. For places like community college, or community theaters, artists and writers and actors aren't "professionals." And maybe that's the biggest difference. Maybe I'm just more comfortable among weirdos and amateurs. Maybe I'm just a weirdo and amateur. This one time after a reading event, one of the other presenters, who I had only just met that night, commented to me that my reading was "so real." That I was "so real." And I'm still u sure what they meant by that. All of this means to say, that I appreciate and would agree with your statement about culture showing up in unexpected places, the idea of finding the jewel, or the diamond, in the rough.

I do want to mention that in the last few years one bright shiny spot for me has been the writing community in Spokane: Spark Central, and the anthologies that Sharma Shields has published, her press, Scablands Books, the Pie & Whiskey reading series, Sam Ligon and Kate Lebo, GetLit!, *The Inlander*, and Carolyn Lamberson from the *Spokesman-Review*, the Summer Stories series, and Auntie's Books. I also was honored to have been asked to write a poem for the Create Health campaign with Terrain and

The Black Lens. And of course, the libraries have been creating some great programs that I've been lucky to have been a part of.

I could not agree more and will be sitting right next to you at the Weirdos and Amateurs Club! On another note, some of the most poignant moments throughout the book occur in relationship to the No Dakota Access Pipeline actions that began in early 2016 on your familial reservation of Standing Rock. These moments address the inaction of leading Democrats, President Obama and Secretary Clinton, as Indigenous water protectors and allies were attacked by local, state, and national law enforcement (in partnership with the private security firm TigerSwan). Before we conclude this interview, I'd love to ask you: when national media attention was directed elsewhere by the election of Trump and the never-ending stream of nightmares that ensued, what happened at Standing Rock?

Midge

If winter hadn't shown up and life hadn't interfered, there'd probably still be a bustling encampment. In February 2017, authorities cleared the camps. Factions of activists went on to fight against other pipelines in construction. People who were arrested dealt with the courts, or served jail terms. The details concerning the Dakota Access Pipeline can be confusing, unless one is familiar with law procedure and terminology. Currently, the pipeline is in use, oil still flows through the line, despite a federal judge revoking a permit and ordering an environmental assessment, last year. You can learn more about it here.

And of course there are recently published books that I highly recommend, such as *Our History Is the Future: Standing Rock Versus the Dakota Access Pipeline*, and the *Long Tradition of Indigenous Resistance* by Nick Estes, and *Standoff: Standing Rock,* the *Bundy Movement*, and the *American Story of Sacred Lands* by Jacqueline Keeler.

Peaches *and* **Above the Hearth**

Rachel Brown

The last time I saw her
as herself,
she was beating softened butter into eggs,
aggressively against the sides of the white bowl.

I was measuring sugar and flour with a knife,
ensuring evenness. Exacting and patient,
she would double check every
measured thing. We had done this
many times, our
system never changing.

She had it all—the flour sugar brown and white baking soda chocolate chips—
in repurposed pickle jars—her home full
of repurposed things.
I eased soda out of the box, flat smooth on the tsp.
She announced that might be her last year-
of christmas cookies, gumdrop cake.

She called my name from her chair as I sliced a gumdrop in half.
I don't remember much after that.

                    *

I miss canned peaches, in white ceramic bowls,
eaten under a pear tree, fresh green grass.
I asked my mother if she knew
how to can peaches.

        yes, she said,
        but,
        no.

I have derailed before,
but nothing prepared me
for a life without peaches,
in mason jars, repurposed.

I sat in her kitchen
yellow countertop before me,
further and further
from the perfect golden globes
        of peaches,
        home.

the oasis of secret dairy queen onion rings
eaten in laughter and the smooth scales
of wild salmon, heavy in novice hands.

the squeeze of dirty fingers on greasy clamps
building low forts above growing crowns and the
soft clink-clink of a cookie jar lid replaced
without stealth, stolen cookies in each hand and third
hidden in the breast pocket.

the golf channel on low, narrated between
snores on sunday afternoons and crab boiled in a gravel driveway
beside the vegetable garden in full bloom and
purple fingers licking blackberry cobbler
on july nights.

teaching small fingers to tie small laces on warm
couch cushions and black pepper evenly,
heavily spread across dinner plates

a stuffed king salmon mounted above the woodstove
a warm hearth.

Screened cage used in artificially attracting Dendroctonus brevicomis.
Jenny Creek, Oregon. 1922.

Hoarding Secrets

Lisa Chen

"As long as you keep secrets and suppress information, you are fundamentally at war with yourself... The critical issue is allowing yourself to know what you know."

—*Bessel A. van der Kolk*, The Body Keeps the Score

My mother hoarded secrets. She whispered some to me in the months leading up to her death, but mostly took them with her. Her secrets were her one true possession; she recounted them in her sleep. When I was a child, I laid next to her at night and kept still as her body tossed in a trance. Before bed, she'd rub Tiger Balm on her shoulder blades, pressing in for relief. Camphor and menthol to end the day and start her restless sleep.

In those days, my mother could neither let her secrets go nor bury them deep enough. They curled around her shoulder blades, balled into neat bundles, keeping her from standing up straight.

No one ever asked a 5'3" Taiwanese woman her thoughts, let alone her secrets, so Ma simply let them curve her into a new shape.

This is where I get my poor posture.

I tried to ask her for some secrets. Especially after the stage four diagnosis. By the time she went to a doctor, the cancer had already spread into her bones and seeped into her lungs and chest.

She was never a forthcoming person. Sometimes she met my questions with silence. But decent sushi and cheap sake got her to speak a little faster, and certainly with less restraint. As if she wanted the cadence of her speech to carry her off her feet to the other side of release.

Ma, what was your first job?
9 years old. I weaved baskets and furniture at a neighborhood shop with your Amá, 阿媽.

My grandmother slapped my mother's knuckles if she fiddled too much, so as not to waste any time. The shop owner gave her candy in the afternoon lull when Amá wasn't looking. Dried sour plum that stuck to your teeth and made you thirsty. My mother earned candy; my Amá earned an extra hand at work.

Why did you leave Taiwan?
A man.
I was young, probably your age. 30.
He was much older.
I thought I was in love.
Sips sake.
I was pregnant.
My coworker said he had a wife back home.
Leans back.
I could not show my face at work again.

My mother spent her twenties as a hostess in nightclubs in Taipei. She convinced her younger sister to join her and leave their sleepy town for the sounds of the big city.

If the nightclub cut hours, which they almost always did, my mother and her sister made a living as tour guides for Japanese tourists. Sisters who sang karaoke on the charter bus for middle-aged Japanese businessmen. Men who smoked cigars and slicked their hair back with greasy oil. The sisters recited simple Japanese phrases and learned to say, arigato gozaimasu, with a deep bow after getting tipped. The men cackled at the concession.

Her pregnancy never came to full-term. A friend of a friend knew what to do, so she did it, is all she ever said.

Continue with more questions, before the sake wears off.

Do you remember when you were taken away to the hospital?
Yes, do you?
Yes.
But you were just a kid.
I still remember.
I was just sad, I'm not sad anymore. Are you sad, Lisa?

Except she never really uses the word sad. She uses other words around it, because in my elementary-level Mandarin, there is no "sad" between us. It is only: not *happy*, *tired*, or *not comfortable*. But deep, deep sadness, it's not a commonly used word between us.

She sucks her teeth.
No more questions, she says.

—◇—

I am 11 years old.

There are many rules here. Turn on and off the light switch before entering the bathroom. Count to three before entering. Knocking is not enough because one of the girls, Allison, is deaf. She'll holler, "Someone's in here." Otherwise, you can open the door. There are no locks here.

You must sign in and out from the clothes bank if you want to wear different clothes than the ones you arrived in. This trading system lets all the girls have a chance to wear the new clothes from donations. I like the maroon-striped top with a scoop neck and a thin white bow on the chest pocket. What goes in such a small pocket? An older girl, Jasmine, is wearing it. She doesn't notice me noticing her. She is asking the counselor for something I do not yet know to ask for. I'm eventually told four other girls are waiting for this top. I put my name down just in case I'm still here.

"Do you have your period?" the counselor asks.
No, not yet.
"Well, if you do, let one of us know, and you'll get one pad at a time. We're running low."
I nod.
I don't want to get my period for the first time in a bathroom where I have to turn the lights on and off before entering.

I'm shown my room. Two twin beds pushed against the cream brick walls. A yellow-stained towel and grey blanket are folded at the foot of the bed. The fluorescent lights hurt my eyes.

"Your roommate just left," the counselor says, "but a new girl will come soon. They always do."

There are no doors here. Later that night, I hear a mix of giggles and other girls crying. What kind of girl giggles in an emergency youth shelter?

The kind of girl I want to be.

I have trouble sleeping here. I wonder how my mother is doing. I told the counselor she tried to swallow her sorrow in sedatives, so I called 9-1-1. They had no next of kin to release me to. I wonder if my mother is sleeping or if she has rubbed her shoulder blades raw by now? I wonder how long I'm here for, if I will learn to laugh as loudly as some of these girls do.

—<o>—

I have dreams about eating my fallen teeth. They are rotten and crunchy. I choke on the sharp edges, but somehow still chew my way through more teeth. I cannot tell you if these are my teeth. Correction: I do not want to know if these are not my teeth. But this dream keeps haunting me. It finds a home in the back of my molars. My palms sweat and I'm forced to chew the lining of my cheeks, until I taste metal. Taste the blood that comes with rotten teeth.

I tell my mother, I have dreams about eating my fallen teeth. She doesn't meet my eyes, and only mumbles back to me, "Me too, my dear, me too."

Except she never calls me *my dear*.

—<o>—

I am 7 years old.

What do you call this flower in English?
I don't know.
My mother laughs her incredulous laugh.

What do they teach you in school then?
They teach me other words. But mostly numbers.

They should teach you the names of flowers.

I laugh.
I will not learn the names of flowers, Ma.

Well, you should.

—<o>—

My mother chose Lily as her American name. She immigrated to the U.S. on a tourist visa. A seven-day bus tour of O'ahu. From one island to another. She had no intention of returning to Taiwan.

She booked a flight from Honolulu to San Diego because a friend of a friend had a job for her. Why is it always a friend of a friend? My mother was a dishwasher in a Chinese restaurant, the Golden Daisy. It stood hidden in a strip mall that has since been torn down. A red awning to represent good fortune. They served complimentary egg drop soup with every meal.

She met my father at this restaurant. He was a waiter. I once found his name tag in my mother's red plastic sewing kit. Black embossed text on a white rectangle—BEN. I don't know why he chose Ben for his American name, but at some point, he was a man who wore a name tag to work.

Two undocumented Taiwanese immigrants find love over food that is not theirs.

When the restaurant was slow, they sold clocks in flea markets. Learned 'two for ten dollars' and 'thank you' in Spanish and English. Carried cash from their tips in white envelopes for exact change. Every second and fourth Sunday, my parents drove to Los Angeles for a larger flea market. A friend of a friend had an extra table for them to sell at.

The drive took over five hours. In the late 1980s, Immigration and Naturalization Services (INS) made surprise inspection checkpoints along major freeways in Southern California to police undocumented migrants. Yellow traffic signs of a family holding hands fleeing across the freeway with the word—CAUTION—peppered Interstate 5. My parents learned from others who were not so lucky. They took local streets to Los Angeles and listened closely for tips about checkpoints. Three a.m. departures to make sure they were not seduced by the convenience of a freeway.

—<o>—

I am 18 months old.

Daddy dies of a heart attack. Brown alcohol made his heart rupture at the age of 36, leaving my mother alone with her secrets.

"Help me, Ma," she says.

My grandmother picked me up at the Taoyuan Airport near Taipei. Unaccompanied minor on EVA Air flight 381. Families were able to wait in the terminal then. Amá heard my wailing as soon as the gate opened.

I wonder what story the airline attendants told themselves about me. If the passengers stirred in their sleep from my cries. What my mother dreamt of in the time away from me, if she found a resting place for her grief or if she stuffed it in for keeps.

I spent two years in Taiwan.

Learned the smells of Amá's kitchen.

Took my first steps with Akong.

Said Amá instead of Ma.

—◇—

In total, Ma worked in restaurants for 44 years. Each day she lifted trays and stacked dishes, wiped tables and bar tops clean. She worked the lunch, dinner, and late night happy hour shifts. Sometimes she did a split shift; naps at 2 p.m. before staff meals. She learned to stay quiet when a customer yelled for her manager and she learned to laugh it off when a flirty customer asked for her.

Over time, my mother tried to let go of her secrets. She liked to take walks in the neighborhood, clip flowers to place in old jars for display. She liked to cook simple meals, make 番茄炒蛋 or tomato egg stir-fry, never on a restaurant's menu but always a home cook's staple. Slice garlic and green onions into neat piles and stir-fry seasoned eggs and tomatoes over rice. She liked to cover her mouth when she laughed and make for loud cackles. My mother tried to bury her secrets, until it was time for new ones.

Ma kept her stage four breast cancer diagnosis from me for more than eight months. In her slow decline, she didn't tell me when she was in pain or if she couldn't eat that day. Whether she slept the night before or felt her steps begin to slow. She didn't tell me what side effects the medication gave or when she stopped taking them altogether. She didn't want to tell me that the medical shower seat felt clunky, so she sat flat in the bath tub for fear of falling. She was hesitant to say that her fingers stopped curling, so gripping chopsticks became a pain and spoons were the convenient way.

We lived together a few times, but in the end, she wanted her privacy. I try to tell myself that my mother just wanted some time alone, some time alone with her secrets.

The last time we lived together, we'd take walks in the Arboretum when she could still take walks. Clip flowers I didn't know the names of on our way home. Do it all over again the next day.

I've tried to learn to let go of the secrets I don't know. The ones I didn't get to ask her about, the ones she never intended to reveal, and the ones she always wanted to tell but didn't.

I wish I told her some of my secrets. Ones I don't even think are secrets anymore.
The times I thought I was in love.
When I lost myself in men and forgot the women who raised me.
And when I, too, sought advice from a friend and took care of a pregnancy.

Three days before my mother passed, I whispered to her, "We did the best we could, Ma." She was heavily sedated and immoble but gave a visible nod.

This was our last exchange.

Fire dispatcher at Cascade, Payette National Forest, Idaho. 1931.

coping mechanism *and* **How will you begin?**

Patrycja Humienik

coping mechanism

gripping the silken
machinery of language. assemblage of
fictions. how they make shelter. construct
sky almost-violet. vibrant only at the edges.

if you could see the edge. you would climb there.
i nearly did myself. having wanted to erase
shitty memories. so wanting ravages me. see

how wretched wanting can be.
the storm seizing cars, entire houses, ancient trees
from the puckering earth. what does it say about me
that i can picture myself there, held by air, watching.

Left foot into the stirrup, swing my right leg over

Larkspur, jonquil, rhododendron

Sing the second song that comes to mind; slip the first into memory's crater

Beeswax & myrrh

Demand the fog tell how

Feel myself a stone at the bottom of a well—no, the sea

Rinse

It has to do with extremities

Don't mention nightmares

Throw open the curtains the way my mother did, perhaps her mother & her mother before

Go to the lake

Arrange the fragments in something like a vase

Believing

Woven at the Center

Katie Lee Ellison

On my last visit to my parents' house before I stopped going home, I sat at the edge of my childhood bed and used my feet to measure the width of a red swastika on the floor. Woven at the center of a mostly white rug, the symbol's outer edges met at the edge of my little toes. On the mattress where I used to fool around with my lanky, blonde high school boyfriend, I imagined filling the negative space between the swastika's crooked arms with more red to create an almost-circle. I considered what I had on hand that could stain red. My blood, I thought, like when I was eleven and marked our living room couch after sitting for what I knew was too long, because I didn't want to think about the blood coming from between my legs or the ways my body needed tending. So I bled onto the white cushions watching the safely plotted lives of characters flashing through our 13-inch TV.

My final trip home was Thanksgiving weekend. Before the guests arrived, my mother rolled up the rug from under my old bed like any other lie, and leaned it in the closet next to my old Jessica McClintock glittered prom dress.

"We don't want anyone getting the wrong idea," she said about my father's rug, smirking and with a tone that implied an obligatory complicity—hers or mine or both, I didn't know.

My mother hid the rug from our old neighbors with whom I used to run in the grass and flick roly-polies; my sister's godparents and godsister whom we'd seen for every Easter, Thanksgiving, and Christmas since she was born; and Oliver, who worked with my parents before I was born. My father defended himself.

"It's Native," he said to me. "Navajo I think."

I've read the swastika represents many things in Navajo culture, including healing, well-being, and auspiciousness. I remember afternoons my father listened to recordings of Lakota chants, bulged his eyes, and said the music made him feel wild. I was a little girl when he listened on our old stereo, yelling and bouncing in imitation of a ceremony he may or may not have ever seen. Watching, I thought I felt what he did, and wanted to bounce with him, make our own ceremony, and release whatever I knew we carried—but my father would not name his burden, hiding it in this culture not ours, so I feared a nameless thing. I ran from the living room to the kitchen to the dining room to his dancing body, and threw a punch at his arm to call him back and keep him from imagining himself somewhere I would never find him.

DNA gave me his strong hands, my mother's slender feet, and Jewish blood, the last of which my father denied via Catholic holy water, baptism, and my mother's mostly Irish Catholic family, though they too had Jews hiding behind changed names. Before the results of a DNA test, my deliberate shift from Christmas to Yom Kippur, Easter to Passover, and long before this writing, my father made clear we were not Jewish.

People hide in plain sight sometimes. People hide us, too, and we let them. Like when I slept over my father's rug.

In sleep, we shed dead skin, produce oil, dream, soothe psychic complications, recuperate bones and muscles, repair wounds, grow hair and nails, and if we're young, we get longer and wider and rounder. My body did this work for one night over a rug belonging to a culture not mine and over a symbol I knew meant evil the way I knew the McDonalds "M" meant French fries. Despite the swastika's global appearance dating as far back as 15,000 years ago and its universal meaning of good luck, German nationalists managed to usurp and change its meaning in the early twentieth century. By 1920, Hitler "understood instinctually that there had to be a symbol as powerful as the hammer and sickle," wrote Steven Heller in *The Swastika: Symbol Beyond Redemption?*, a book I was assigned to copyedit for re-release in my first job at a small publishing house after college. I gifted the book to my father that Christmas, knowing his "love for the aesthetics" of the swastika, as he used to explain.

That last night at my parents' home, my dead skin fell onto the rug and my dreams mixed with all it brought into the room. In waking hours, I insisted my dreams were not tied to my father's. I attempted to believe that because this rendering of the swastika on the floor didn't speak German or even English, but a Native language neither I nor my father knew, that it was safe.

Best case scenario, the rug was my father's attempt to reclaim the symbol. If made by brown hands and laid at the center of his oldest daughter's former bedroom, it no longer meant he was dirty or that he should never have been born. It became his to name, or so I believe his story goes. Except that he spoke German, watched World War II on the History Channel every other weekend, and hid a rifle in his closet.

His story about the rug was a delusion.

To rest with a swastika in the room, keep attention on the white of the rug around it. The white walls, the white sheets. Deny, suspend reality, and corroborate that the family isn't Jewish, that loyalty is paramount, that the love within these walls is unconditional. To sleep over a swastika, erase its meanings, believe it clean as his dry skin from all the Ivory soap, pray, like in the Twelve-Step meetings, nevermind the prescriptions in the master bedroom drawers, the silenced obsession with all these lies.

Here's something: The earliest appearance of the swastika was as a symbol of fertility carved into a mammoth tusk discovered in present-day Ukraine—the same territory that claims the towns where my father's Jewish ancestors were born.

In India, the symbol is still hung over door frames for good luck, but on my old bedroom floor in Los Angeles, it was a weapon. No blood I shed on the white would change it to a circle nor erase my father's disgust for our blood and our bones.

My father didn't want us to survive as we are, but as something else. Something we'll never be.

Getting out of bed that morning, I was careful not to place my bare feet on the swastika for fear that it would break our home open. As a girl, the Southern California earthquakes, fires, droughts; the smoke-billowing during the '92 uprising, police beatings, car races out our windows in the dark morning hours, and car chases every sun-bleached afternoon on the news; the violent fights, slamming phones, and pills hidden in purses and bathrooms: these had me waiting for the day our walls would fall. The fear carried through to adulthood when I imagined touching my flesh to the red of that tainted symbol could release the rage of generations, not just of our family, but of those who made the rug and sold it or lost it to white men who knew nothing of them, those who lost the land where our house stood, those from our past who followed us, called for us to hear them.

I woke to the swastika before my mother rolled it up on Thanksgiving morning, sat on the edge of the bed, and considered pressing my toes to it—the symbol of peace, good tidings, abundance, murder, hatred. I considered our house falling, attic roof to basement floor, from the weight of my body on it, our pressure point. I imagined all I could set loose in the destruction.

Car Camping Outside Livingston, MT

Kate Garcia

We lay there rigid and calculating how best to siphon
heat from the dog's febrile little body. My feet have been sacrificed
to a frenzied cold.   Hours

earlier we'd played cribbage and drank beers and faced West
into a coiled pool of fruit sap settling   tethers
between earth and elsewhere pulling inward becoming taught. I wished I hadn't said

that thing about you not being so affectionate
lately because the silence unmoored me.
Now I have to pee.

I shift my stiff body forward released from
a suffocation of duvet and sleep smells   toward the car door
rocking with the weather. Dropping down onto the wet earth is like

being born into a static chasm   sharp soil polyps
tattooing the bottom of my bare feet.   The space between
body and sod all choked up.

The plain is dusted blue black and grey   Southward
mountains are blackhole shadow beacons   backlit slices
cut from felted clouds.

Crouched down naked from waist to ankles I look out
into the pall of dead grass   endless and unburdened
by trees, rocks, anything. The wind burrows down my eardrums

waking me from the belly outward.   I wonder if you ever think about
when we lived in that big Portland house together   the
one with two beds – we followed each other

back and forth all night long. I wonder what you think about.
You are a product of light   that is a product of darkness.
I stand up   redress   lean against the solitary metal beast.

$23.00 a Night

Jaton Rash

When the sheriff's deputy came to the duplex to enforce the eviction, I was busy moving my family's belongings onto a narrow strip of grass just outside our door. I was working alongside one of the landlord's maintenance men and a teenage boy who I assumed was his son. I wanted everything to be as neat and orderly as possible and I quietly went about hauling the boxes outside and stacking them up in piles. The two others did more or less the same. It was mid-morning on an early November day in 1997. The deputy came into the duplex and looked around, then down at the court directive in his hand. "Where's the son?" he asked Stan, the maintenance man. Stan nodded in my direction. I must have seemed harmless enough, because the deputy didn't say anything to me.

My parents were outside, standing next to the growing pile of stuff. They were anxious, ready to go—but where? My sister had found someone willing to take her and her two-year-old daughter in, and they had already gone. So my parents and I were left to manage the situation on our own. I organized our collection of boxes and clothes and garbage bags full of stuff while my dad waited for an acquaintance of his, a man named Nick, to come over and help us move everything to a storage unit down the street. My mom was standing, holding onto her purse, trying not to cry. She had been on the phone earlier in the morning, trying to find a place for us to stay, and had eventually found a family friend willing to take us in for a night.

We had a lot of stuff in our little two-bedroom duplex, a strange fact considering that my parents and my sister were addicted to heroin and had sold most anything of value to support their addictions. Somehow, the place was still stuffed. We had held onto kitchen wares, furniture, clothes and knick-knacks, beds, and my niece's crib and toys. And now it was all heaped up in a pile on the grass.

Of my two parents, my dad was the more animated that morning. Nick was late, and my dad was getting increasingly anxious. He stood in the parking lot expecting Nick to drive up at any moment, and from time to time he went out to the street looking for the car, hoping that by looking he could summon it faster. When he wasn't pacing the parking lot, he watched Stan and his son carry the last of our things out of the duplex.

"I don't have a lot of sympathy for you guys," Stan said. "I see four adults not working."

"Shut up, fat boy," my dad responded, just loud enough for Stan to hear. Stan didn't say anything back. This insult was unusual; I had never known my dad to resort to childish name-calling. Stan was a big guy and at least a decade younger than my dad, who was past fifty and not in the best shape. If there had been a fight, my dad probably would have lost.

Nick finally showed up sometime around noon. He was a disagreeable old man with a full head of white hair who did yard work around the city to make ends meet. His car rolled into the parking lot and he gave my dad the bad news: the car was full. He had bought some power tools and other things that morning and there wasn't room for anything else, so he wouldn't be able to help us like he'd said he would. He started driving away, but my dad stopped him. They talked for a moment, then Nick agreed to put some of our things on top of the car and move them that way. So that's what happened: I helped place a box or two on top of the car, and then Nick drove slowly to the storage unit, about five blocks away. My dad followed on foot.

Nick returned for two more trips before he had to leave. Amazingly, none of the boxes fell off the car. My mom gave Nick a hug and a kiss on the cheek for his efforts.

Our pile of belongings was smaller now, but there was still a lot left over. My parents and I lingered for a bit longer. Without any way to move the rest of the things to the storage unit, it was becoming clear that we would have to leave them. I was having a hard time with this concept. I wanted to stay and guard everything, but my dad was anxious to leave. In fact, both of my parents were anxious, and not just because of the eviction and the pile of stuff on the grass. They were anxious for their afternoon fix. My dad probably had enough for a fix in his shoulder bag, but there was still the issue of finding a place to shoot up.

My dad came up with an idea: there was an abandoned shopping cart on the side of the street nearby—why not use that to take more stuff down to the storage unit? The suggestion was aimed at me. I wasn't thrilled about the idea, but I also didn't want to leave our stuff. I loaded up the shopping cart with some books, tools, and other items—a fraction of what was still there—and left the Copperfield Apartments with my parents for the last time. We took a right on Kauffman Avenue and headed toward the storage unit, my parents a pace or two in front of me. Behind us was our old neighborhood, a collection of modest houses and low-rent apartments uphill from the rail yard. We had moved here to the west side of Vancouver, Washington from a nice house on the east side of town about a year and a half earlier.

The traffic was light on Kauffman Avenue that day and there weren't many people around. When my parents and I came to the gravel road that led to the storage facility, we parted ways. The plan was to meet up at the library in the evening and then go to the place my mom had lined up for us. It was a lady named Phyllis, a friend of my grandma's, who had agreed to take us in for a night, though she had little idea who we were.

I pushed the shopping cart to the front gate of the storage facility, punched in the code to get in, and continued on to the unit. The storage unit was fairly spacious and only about one-third full. There were family pictures, posters and prints my dad had kept from when he was a printer, bags of clothes, blankets and other bedding material, and my baseball card collection. I added to the pile the things I had brought down in the shopping cart.

From the storage facility I walked a couple of miles to the library. I was carrying a green duffel bag my sister had given me with yellow lettering that said *US Forest Service Alaska Region*. I had stuffed some clothes and a small radio into the bag. At the library, I flipped through magazines for a while and when I got tired, I folded my arms on the table and put my head down on them, just like I used to do at my desk in high school. I didn't know what to expect. I didn't know if my parents would show up like they said, and I didn't have a plan for what I would do if they didn't. I was twenty and should have been able to take care of myself, but to be honest I was pretty helpless at that point. I had no vehicle or job and nowhere to go.

When evening came, my parents did show up and we caught a bus to Phyllis's house in east Vancouver. Phyllis lived alone in a spacious, well-kept, two-story house. She was a kind lady with a round, friendly face who knew my grandma from when they both volunteered at a food bank. I had met Phyllis before, but it was long before and I can't imagine she recognized me. I don't think she had ever met my parents before.

That evening we all sat in the living room, watching TV. Phyllis and my dad made small talk about the job market. They agreed it was tough out there for a person looking for a job. My mom and dad each made a phone call. My mom called a relative in California to ask if he could help us out, but she couldn't reach him. My dad called a motel and asked what the rates were. Later in the evening Phyllis excused herself from the living room. While she was gone, my dad said to my mom, "Did you see those books upstairs? Those are worth something."

"Are you serious?" I snapped, summoning the most disapproving voice I could muster. He responded only with a sly grin. He was half-serious, at least. Phyllis rejoined us and we all continued watching TV until bedtime.

My bedroom for the night was upstairs. The small room had a wood floor and was furnished with only a bed and a nightstand. Under different circumstances the room might have felt cozy, but on that night, it was cold and a little creepy. There weren't enough blankets on the bed to keep warm, and in any case, my mind was crowded with worry and distraction, so I got only four or five hours of light sleep. Back at the duplex, I'd been sleeping on a sofa, and there had been no electricity and little food as eviction day approached, but all the same, I knew I would have slept better there, because it was home.

We left Phyllis's house the next morning and walked to Mill Plain Boulevard to catch a bus downtown. Our plan for the day was much like the day before: I would wait at the library while my parents took care of business. Then they would show up later on and the three of us would figure out what to do next.

I'm not sure where my parents went, but it must have been someplace where my dad could panhandle, a supermarket parking lot maybe. He would approach people in parking lots and tell a brief hard-luck story—then ask for money. He was good at this and would only get better in the months to come. My mom didn't panhandle, so she probably waited somewhere, in a fast-food place or on a park bench, until my dad had enough money to score a bag of heroin. On that day he needed to make even more money than usual, because he wanted to get us into a motel room that night.

I put in a long day at the library, longer than the day before. I spent time sitting on one of the sofas, flipping through magazines. After a while I went behind the library and sat on some bleachers next to a baseball field. I ate some crackers that were in my bag and tuned into sports talk on the radio. I believe it was Jim Rome, the brash, hyper-macho talk show host who was on air for several hours each morning. "Have a take, don't suck," was the advice he always gave to his callers. I listened to him a lot back then, even though I knew his show was junk food for the mind. After my break I went back into the library for more waiting. The library was an easy place to wait; it was spacious, the sofas in the magazine section were comfortable, and it was open until 8:00 p.m.

My parents came to get me in the evening. We stopped in the lobby on our way out so my dad could use the pay phone. He called a motel to ask if there were any vacancies, and there were—so long as he had enough money, there was a place we'd be able to stay that night. In the bright lights of the lobby, I could see that my dad's eyes were jaundiced. I wanted to ask him what was wrong, but I stayed silent.

We headed toward downtown, which wasn't far. The weather was mild, perfect for an early evening stroll. There was almost a sense of camaraderie among us—we were in this together and there wasn't really any choice but to be kind to each other and just let things happen as they would. My dad was the leader of our little group, but he seemed uncertain about where he was leading us.

When we got downtown, we caught a bus to a neighborhood called Hazel Dell, a few miles to the north. In Hazel Dell, we got off the bus and crossed the street to the Value Motel, a large motel and apartment complex next to I-5. My mom and I lingered outside the office while my dad paid for the cheapest room available. The price was $21 plus tax, for a total of about $23. As we walked to our room, my dad told us what the office had told him: only two people were allowed to stay in the room. Clearly, we would be ignoring this rule, but as it turned out, it wasn't strictly enforced.

When I walked into the room, I understood why there was a two-person rule—it was tiny. There was a bed, a sink and nightstand, a TV and a shared bathroom. Tears welled up in my eyes as I realized I would be staying the night here. My parents didn't seem to be as put off by the size of the room as I was.

My dad went to Burger King that first night to get dinner, which was a Whopper for each of us. We ate, watched a little TV, and then it was bedtime. I curled up on the floor with a blanket from the bed set. The next morning, we were up and out before the 11:00 check-out time.

My parents went off to do their thing and I wandered into Hazel Dell with my duffel bag. I walked into an upscale trailer park and sat down on a park bench. It wasn't clear when or how I would get back in touch with my parents. I decided to hang out in the vicinity of the motel and hope that they would return and that my dad would get another room that night. This was the third day of homelessness. I hadn't slept well for days and food was an uncertainty. My ability to think clearly was diminishing.

I reconnected with my parents that afternoon and we got into a room once again. My dad bought Taco Bell for dinner that night. Soon, he started making enough money panhandling to pay for two nights on the room each time he went to the office, so we didn't have to check out in the morning. We would just have to move aside when the housekeeper came in to empty the trash and vacuum and replace the drinking glasses with new ones. My parents and I gradually settled into our new lives at the motel.

My sister and her daughter began staying in a room at the motel about a month later. My sister had taken up panhandling by then. She and my dad went out each day to supermarket parking lots and other places to plead for money. They grew closer to each other in the months that followed. My mom and I drew inward, staying in the motel room together drinking the beer and wine that she stole from local stores and eating snacks we both stole from the Fred Meyer supermarket across the street from the motel. We sometimes babysat my niece while my sister was out there in the wild, hustling.

My family's misfortune accelerated over the next year. My mom, my sister and I were each arrested in separate incidents. My dad never got arrested but he did get his jaw broken when he was punched by a fellow addict. At various points, other members of our extended family tried to help out: grandparents, an aunt, an uncle. When my grandparents came to the motel, they said that they didn't recognize my dad right away, so changed was his appearance.

By the summer my dad was getting worn down by the panhandling routine and was making less money than before. Sometimes he could find a church or charitable organization to pay for the motel room for a night or two, or even for a week in one case. But other times he didn't have enough money to pay for two consecutive nights, so he and my mom and I would have to drag our stuff down to a stairwell at the end of the hallway and stash it there for the afternoon. My mom would hang out around the motel and I would either do the same or go for a long walk. My dad would appear later in the afternoon or early evening and pay for a room, and we would gather our stuff from the stairwell.

These motel room evictions happened many times that summer. On the mornings when we had to vacate, my parents and I would quietly clear out our room with a shared sense of duty. We were still together, but our unity was fraying. My dad had wondered aloud once or twice why he couldn't have the room to himself, considering that he was the only one paying for it.

In July I got a job as a school custodian. After a couple of weeks on the job, I got my first paycheck and opened an account at the bank inside the Fred Meyer by the motel. I was walking through the parking lot, back to the motel, when I ran into my dad. This wasn't exactly a chance encounter. He knew it was payday. He immediately asked if I could give him some money. I said I couldn't, but he wasn't going to give up easily. We walked together to the motel, and in the room, he continued to press me for money. He sat in front of the sink in a green plastic chair, leaning forward. "Come on," he said over and over, and my response each time was, "I can't." With each "I can't," his head bowed down a little.

"I need to save this money if I'm gonna get out of this place," I told him. He didn't have a counterargument; he just kept saying, "Come on." Even after he knew I wasn't going to give in, he kept pleading, but less emphatically: Come on. Finally, he gave up. He didn't kick me out; for another month, I stayed in the room with my parents, paying nothing toward the $23 a day.

In September, I moved out of my parents' room and into my own room at the motel. This wasn't much of a leap, but it put some distance between us. There were several dozen rooms in that part of the motel, so I was never in a room next door to my parents. My sister and her daughter had moved out of the motel months earlier, so I never ended up next door to them, either. I didn't see my parents much after I left their room, but I still bumped into them once in a while.

I followed my dad's example and paid for two nights each time I went to the office. I soon realized that this was a lot of money for such a tiny room, around $700 a month. I applied for one of the on-site apartments that were managed by the motel, but the office didn't get back to me. I was making around $1,000 a month and even though most of that went toward the cost of the room, I was able to save a little. I settled into a new life at the motel, a working life. I was still homeless, but I had achieved a measure of freedom and could begin plotting a way out of the motel.

About two months after I moved into my own room, my mom knocked on my door. I wasn't completely surprised when I saw the shape she was in. She was skinnier than I remembered and seemed to be in a daze. She wanted to stay with me. She and my dad had drifted apart in the couple months since I'd left them. My dad was now staying in a room with his girlfriend Alecia and my mom was staying with a man named Keith who was another permanent resident at the motel. I told my mom that I didn't want her to stay with me. She pleaded with me and when I said no a second time, she gave up and returned to Keith's room.

I stayed at the motel a little longer. On Thanksgiving, I ate dinner at the nearby Denny's and for Christmas dinner, I bought something at a local mini-mart. I was working the swing shift at a high school with about five other custodians and never mentioned to any of them that I was living in a motel—that I was essentially homeless. I moved into a studio apartment in downtown Vancouver just before New Year's, bringing with me one or two grocery sacks full of stuff, my duffel bag and a bicycle. The apartment was an upstairs room in an old house. As at the motel, I shared the bathroom with another room.

My mom left the motel around the same time as me and ended up in Seattle where she briefly lived on the streets. My dad stayed in the Portland area where he lived mostly in motels or on the streets. For a time, he lived with my sister in a dilapidated apartment in north Portland. I often saw him on the bus or on the street. When we ran into each other we would say hi and talk. I would try to keep our conversations brief. As the years went by, I increasingly tried to avoid him when I saw him in public. Once or twice my dad called and left a message on my answering machine. He just wanted to say hi and see how I was doing, and to ask if I knew how my mom was doing.

My family's time in the motel is etched on my mind, but I remember the better times, too—the times before all that. I remember my dad's irreverent sense of humor and all the fishing trips we went on, the times when my mom came home from her job as a housekeeper and made dinner. Before we moved to Vancouver, we had lived in small towns and off-the-map places in western Washington. We were poor, but we enjoyed the charms of those places.

Even at the Value Motel, there were moments of comfort, when my parents and I watched TV together in the evening and talked about what we had done during the day. My dad sometimes told stories about the people he asked for money in the parking lots. Once, there was a young woman who initially refused to give him anything but had a change of heart and came running back with a twenty-dollar bill. Another time, there was a man who listened patiently to my dad's plea but then responded, *Sorry, I don't carry change with me.* And once, there was a man sitting in his truck, working his way through a pile of scratch-it lottery tickets, not having any luck. *I'm getting killed on these things*, he told my dad, before giving him ten dollars.

Displacement Activities

Phillip Barron

for Alberto Blanco

A canvas and nylon neighborhood
of uncertain dimensions begins
at the corner of Burnside and Second
stretching north until the Lan Su
Garden's grouse reaches city hall.
Gardeners wait for work,
lining up for the gates to open
again someday.
               It is hard
to smile without a mouth,
to recognize a friend or even
a grin that is not your brother's.
How long has it been since
every day remained the same?
The concerned concern themselves
with dancing on the edge
of a dollar, and fire hydrants run
dry without a drought

for three years. Weeds batter
the fence that is, for many,
the fourth wall. Two
women debate the law
of excluded middle:
either it is true that a tarp
is a roof and a roof marks a trap
where the sharp edge of self
lines a narrative map, or it isn't.

Donna Miscolta in conversation with Kailee Haong

Spring 2021 · Digital Exchange

I was one of the few people of color in my high school, much like the protagonist of Donna Miscolta's new collection, *Living Color: Angie Rubio Stories.* For me, reading this book was a personal, intimate experience, a peek inside the life of another brown teenager trying to figure out what it all means. I found myself quickly forming a connection with Angie, feeling in her contrasting shyness and boldness a reflection of my own courage and vulnerability. What Miscolta is doing in *Living Color* is painting a closely-observed portrait of life—of growing up, of being a teenager, of moving, of discovering and exploring one's identity, of race relations and familial relations and the cultural significance of both. In our conversation, Miscolta felt like a mentor, a voice I needed to hear when I was younger. We spoke about *Living Color* but also about life, about writing, about brown-ness and "other-ness." It is a conversation I will carry with me for a long time.

Published September 2020 Jaded Ibis Press in, *Living Color* is Miscolta's third work of fiction, and was named by Las Comadres and Friends National Latino Book Club as one of the 2020 Latino Books of the Year. Her story collection *Hola and Goodbye* was published by Carolina Wren Press in 2016, and was the recipient of several awards and honors, including the Doris Bakwin Award for Writing by a Woman, the Independent Publishers award for Best Regional Fiction, and the International Latino Book Award for Best Latino Focused Fiction.

Haong

In your first story collection, *Hola and Goodbye*, you take readers back to the 1920s on the border of California and Mexico. In *Living Color*, you take us to the 60s and 70s in California. I'm interested in the way you establish time and place in your writing, using political and cultural world events to shape the narrative. How was it for you, shifting from writing about a booming time of rebirth like the 20s to the sort of heaviness associated with everything going on in the 60s and 70s?

Miscolta

For me, everything starts with character and imagining that character in a particular space that is defined by a specific time and certain events—for instance, Angie growing up in the 60s and seeing an article in the newspaper about how Sam Cooke and his band were turned away from a hotel in Louisiana, or Angie seeing reports of the Lennon-Ono bed-in on TV. These incidents establish the social and political atmosphere of the time, and while Angie takes note of them, she's also removed from them in the sense that they occur for her on the news and not directly to her. Because the focus of the story is on the relationships among the characters whose conflicts and dramas take place against the backdrop of the larger world but may not directly bump up against or collide with it, I'm also somewhat removed from any emotional burden inherent in the state of the world in which my characters are existing. So shifting among time periods is not an obstacle and can be a diversionary change. And to make it more fun and to find more affinity with the character, I try to connect with a time period by thinking, for instance, of my grandmother as a young woman in the 20s and 30s or my mother in the 40s and 50s for the stories in *Hola and Goodbye* or myself growing up in the 60s and 70s for the stories in *Living Color*. While the two books are distinct, what connects them, I think, is the focus on character, on people living these ordinary lives in pursuit of ordinary dreams but in their own particular set of circumstances.

Haong

Do you see bits and pieces of your grandmother or your mother present in your characters? Do you ever find yourself enmeshing your characters with people in your life?

Miscolta

I do draw on characteristics from people I know to create fictional characters. In *Living Color*, I did draw on some aspects of my mother, which is not to say that my mother is Angie Rubio's mother. What I'm trying to do is create a certain dynamic for the characters, and it's based on relationships. I think it's a common dynamic between adult and child, which is that each is seeing a situation from their particular perspective. Because the adult has the power, their perspective dominates, and the child often feels unheard or invisible. for instance, when Angie is in fourth grade and is informed by one of her classmates that she's in the "dumb class." Angie asks her mother to talk to the principal about moving her to another class. Her mother not only brushes off Angie's request, but she reprimands Angie for getting smart with her. So what you have are two characters, each with their own concern, and the child's concern is missed. When I'm borrowing traits from a person I know, it's to this end, to think about the relationship between the two characters. I always try to think of each character as someone who has his or her own story, whether that story is the main story or not.

Haong

In thinking more about motherhood and how it is discussed and dealt with in *Living Color*, I was especially intrigued by Angie's relationship Nelda, as it feels so different than her relationship with her mother. Nelda refers to Angie as "mija," and this sort of shines through as we see a strong bond being forged between the two of them as the book progresses.

Miscolta

Nelda's a different personality than Angie, and also anyone else in their family as they tend to be more quiet, but Nelda is this brassy character, louder—she teases a lot and is sassy. She believes in herself, even when she doesn't know how to do something. I think this is what draws Angie to her, although Angie is also afraid of her. Angie likes Nelda's frankness, but is also embarrassed by it. When Nelda calls her "mija," it's a term of endearment. It's a way that Angie understands that there is this connection. A lot of times girls growing up will have an adversarial relationship with their mother and it's always nice to have this "other" female figure to look to, where it's not so fraught and there's not the same kind of emotional tension. For me, it was important to have another older female in the story.

Haong

In what ways do you feel a connection or disconnection between your two books?

Miscolta

Alberto Rios, who has authored seventeen books, has said that all his books speak to each other. I like that idea and I think my books are in conversation with each other as well. They deal with similar themes – identity, displacement, belonging, and family relationships. While the stories in Hola and Goodbye provided a picture of what is lost and gained culturally and psychologically over three generations of an immigrant family, Living Color focuses on one family that represents two of those generations and looks closely at the effects of race, class, and assimilation on a young girl and how she responds to and counters them.

Haong

Tell me a little more about California. Angie moves from Hawaii to California at the beginning of the novel when she is very young. What is California to you?

Miscolta

California is where my family from Mexico and my family from the Philippines—two countries colonized by Spain—came together on land that also had once been occupied by Spain. My siblings still live in Southern California and I like going there to visit. It's not really home anymore for me, but it's where my roots in this land begin.

I spent most of my growing-up years in the very southern part of Southern California. We lived in National City, which is just south of San Diego. Except for the two years we lived in Hawaii, San Diego and, more specifically, National City was my world. We never ventured much beyond those boundaries. We were a family of seven and vacations weren't within our means. But I knew a world awaited out there. My frames of reference were the ocean to the west which we visited only on special occasions, Disneyland to the north in Anaheim which we drove to for the day for several summers, the mountains and desert to the east which was like a foreign country to us, and Tijuana to the south which we were given to understand was off limits even though my grandmother shopped there and my grandfather was a regular at the famed Caliente racetrack. And even though there was much of California to see, as a girl, I had somehow become fixed on Oregon because it suggested ruggedness to me and I wanted to be rugged, physically and in spirit, even though I've always been a reedy, shy sort. It turns out I only spent a few months in Oregon after college before heading to Seattle, where, without meaning to, I stayed permanently.

Haong

What truly makes California "home" for Angie?

Miscolta

For Angie, home is a place she has yet to find. In the last pages of the book we know that she is headed away from Kimball Park, but we don't know where. But I think that wherever she ends up, Kimball Park, California will always be a part of who she is. There is no escaping where you're from.

Haong

Were you reading anything at the time of writing *Living Color* that influenced anything about the story or the characters?

Miscolta

I wrote the stories in *Living Color* over a long period of time. Since I'm always reading something it's safe to say that I was probably influenced at some point by somebody. As I read, I like to be immersed in the story so that the craft is invisible to me, but at some level my brain is probably taking note of language and structure, though maybe not in any precise, easily explicable way, but something more nebulous, akin to osmosis.

I will say that I had some time ago read several of Sue Townsend's Adrian Mole books, which I found hilarious and touching. These are written in diary form, so the structure is different from *Living Color*. When I was writing *Living Color*, I can't say whether I was thinking of Adrian Mole, but I also can't see how its influence would have eluded me. I think everything I read sticks with me in some raw, unprocessed way that gets stored and blended with a bunch of stuff that filters out onto the page at opportune moments.

Film can also inspire or confirm my artistic choices. I had written much of *Living Color* when the film Boyhood came out in 2014. When I saw the film, I thought that this is what I was trying to do with Angie Rubio's life—view her at various points of her girlhood. If anything, it validated for me that this form of storytelling was an effective vehicle for examining a life.

Haong

I'm always enthralled by an author's choice in perspective. It's perhaps the first thing you notice when you begin reading a book—and what sets the stage for the tone. Tell me about your decision process in making *Living Color* a close third narration. There were moments where we get so close to Angie, it almost feels like we could slip into first person and get right inside her head, but then we are drawn back into the entire scene and made to look at the bigger picture again. I'd love to hear a little bit about your process behind establishing the book's point-of-view.

Miscolta

Third person has always felt the most natural point-of-view for me to write in. It's usually what appears on the page when I begin writing a story, though I have written first-person POV characters when the story seems to demand it. In several of the stories in *Hola and Goodbye*, the "I" fell onto the page. For the Angie stories, I needed to inhabit her but still separate myself from her character since many of the incidents and events in Angie's life were things that I had experienced or witnessed. I wanted to be sure that I was writing about Angie and not me. Close third-person gave me the flexibility to move inside Angie's head for her thoughts and look through her eyes to observe the world. I could inhabit her, viewing her surroundings with a close, subjective lens, but also with a longer, wider lens that gave a broader, more encompassing, and almost objective perspective. The truth is, for me, often craft choices such as point of view are not deliberate. I tend to feel my way through the writing. If I'm lucky, what results truly serves the story.

We follow Angie through childhood and into adolescence, and witness in each chapter as she "grows up" in some way or another. Was your writing process as linear as the book presents? Did you write the stories chronologically, or did you find yourself jumping around in Angie's life story a bit while writing? Tell me a little bit about your writing process.

Miscolta

The first half dozen or so stories were not written in chronological order. Early on I was just having fun writing about this character at different stages of her life, though I was consciously picking educational grade levels as my reference points. After the first six stories it was clear what I was wanting to do, which was to look at how a young brown girl fares at each of the stages of her education. I was examining my own years as I wrote about Angie's. For each story I thought back to a moment that was notable in some way for me and used it either as the seed from which to grow the story or as a jumping off point to discover a different story. For instance, when I was in the fourth grade, I was told by a classmate that we were in the dumb class. That's a situation that Angie finds herself in and the story "Social Studies" opens with the words, "You know this is the dumb class, don't you?"

In the story "First Confession," Angie finds herself in an embarrassing dilemma because she has promised a big surprise for one of the nuns who is sick. I did something similar when I was that age. But that didn't feel like the story to me, it felt like part of what was leading to the story which was all about lying and truth and faith. That incident that I had taken from real life was not the story, but it helped to shape it.

Haong

I'm also curious as to the specific ages you've chosen to focus on for each chapter. What prompted these particular ages? How did you decide what age was worthy of its own chapter? To me, the choice of age felt calculated—the perfect moments to dip in and out of Angie's life.

Miscolta

The structure of the book is grade by grade. It's a grade by grade look at Angie's education, not necessarily what you learn in class, but what you learn from your peers and how to behave. Each grade deals with a particular year and age of Angie's life. In choosing the events I wanted to write about for Angie, I look back at the things that I experienced while growing up and use those as inspiration for Angie's situation, for instance, the slumber party. I used that experience as a way to make Angie feel both invisible *and* singled out. The events at my slumber party were not the events at Angie's slumber party, but the feelings were the same. That sense of not belonging but also a moment of humiliation and scorn. I think those "perfect moments," as you referred to them are moments of specific emotions. Everything is layered and interconnecting.

Haong

Angie not only faces a lot of physical displacement throughout the novel, but also experiences social displacement, such as not being able to speak the language her parents speak. I know this to be a common experience amongst immigrants and refugees, as my family came to the United States from Cambodia in the 70s and I was never taught to speak Khmer.

Miscolta

The term "generation gap," referring to the difference in outlook between two generations, first came into use when I was growing up in the 60s. Layered upon this gap was, for many immigrant families, is another gap—one over which a language did not cross because parents decided that it was better for children to only learn English, that learning two languages would be confusing, that it was unnecessary to have more than English to be in America.

But language is connection not only to one another, but to a past, and when only some members of a family have access to it, there's a disparity and disequilibrium that happens that goes beyond the parent/child and elder younger differences.

What do you think is the benefit of estranging Angie from her family in this way? In cutting off an entire way of communicating? I've thought a lot about how important non-verbal communication is in these instances.

From a storytelling perspective, I wanted to include this because it's such a common occurrence in immigrant families. Angie's lack of Spanish contributes to her sense of loss and dislocation. It's one more thing that heightens her sense of not belonging. In Angie's family, only her mother and her aunt speak Spanish, which they use to converse with each other, excluding the other members of the family who are often the topic of their conversation. Angie's non-verbal responses are foot-stomping, sighing, and feigned indifference, the rejoinders of any young person to parental offenses.

Your title, "Living Color," feels exactly right. We see color in the very beginning, as Angie's self-awareness for the color of her skin and the color of her classmates' skin permeates her thoughts. This is a ringing motif throughout.

Yes, Angie is immediately aware of what sets her apart from her classmates in her kindergarten classroom. Skin color is forever after a factor in how she sees herself in the context of others because it's how others define her, and their definitions are often negative. To her six-year-old playmates, brown equals monster. In the third grade, she is a brownie in a Brownie uniform, which more than amuses her troop members. In the fourth grade, brown equals the dumb class.

Haong

Nearing the end, we get deep into Angie's interiority as she completes her high school project that is essentially writing diary entries that correspond with certain colors. Tell me about what you hope readers might gain from reading Angie's color assignment.

Miscolta

Colors have definitions and this is what Angie decides to explore as she sits down to write the dreaded assignment of writing her autobiography. She gets the idea of associating events in her life with a particular color from one of the paintings she studies in an art gallery as part of the assignment on her class cultural trip to Los Angeles. She observes Gainsborough's *Blue Boy* and the characteristics and mood the color blue imbues its subject. She feels inadequate to the assigned task of writing her autobiography in a straigh forward way, so she chooses to see her life's events and her feelings about them as colors. A life and a person are more than the color of her skin. For Angie, learning to ride a bike evoked the color blue, often seen as a tranquil color or one of sadness. But it could also be flight and freedom. Green could mean verdant hills, but it could also be associated with the truth of one's self. These are the sorts of things Angie reckons with and discovers as she views her life in living color.

Haong

I like to look for turning points with regard to character development when I'm reading. Something that really stuck out to me was how pivotal Angie's high school trip to Los Angeles was for her. In the first half of the book, or three-quarters, really, Angie is a bit of a loner. She has friends here and there but focuses so much on how un-alike she is from everyone, even her family members. When we follow Angie on this trip, there comes a moment where she simply decides she does not care if she is alone or not. What is this breaking point? Is it simply maturity, growing up? How do we move from little timid wants-to-fit-in Angie to this fully formed teenager who can sit with her loneliness and make something of it?

Miscolta

The assignment she and her classmates are given in eleventh grade to write their autobiography seems ridiculous to Angie, since she feels she has yet to live her life, to do interesting things, to see things and to be seen in a way that fully acknowledges her as a person. It's the trip to Los Angeles and this glimpse of the world outside of Kimball Park where she has lived for much of her life that opens up the world a bit for her and helps her to examine her life, her perceptions of her place within her family, her peers, and in the world as far she knows and understands it. It starts with the Gainsborough painting during the museum visit and with each activity on the trip, there is an accumulation of insight and tiny epiphanies about who she has been, who she is now, and that to get someplace beyond her boundaries, she needs to be a little bit bolder. And that comes with risks, which she accepts.

Haong

I loved the line "Someday, she promised herself, she would narrate her own story." We see the writer's hand here for just a moment, dipping in to sort of give us a wink, to say, "I told you she'd write her own story."

Do you envision the completion of this assignment for Angie to be an epiphany? Was this autobiography the beginning of her narrating her own story? I feel this assignment instilled a confidence in her writing she had not yet truly unlocked.

Miscolta

Even though I was looking at each story as standing on its own, of course there is an inherent arc in the story when taken as a whole. Plus, in the grade by grade telling of Angie's story, with each year she has a little more self-awareness, a little more courage to act. In the story in which she has to write an autobiography, it's the first time she takes a trip away from Kimball Park to Los Angeles, and she has a glimpse of a bigger world and the slightest sense of the possibilities that could open up for her. Angie has sort of balked at this task. How does a sixteen-year-old write an autobiography? So she connects things with colors. I think this assignment is the beginning of her recognizing that words are a path to someplace. The feedback she gets from her teacher is that her approach had been different, but it had been provocative and bold, so Angie latches onto those words. She adopts those words as her motto.

Haong

At the end of the book, I wanted to envision Angie today, faced with the complications of this world we live in—racial disparity, the struggle for equality, and classism still abound. How do you see Angie fitting into our present-day reality?

Miscolta

At this point in her life, I think Angie would be tired of the fight, not that she would give up. She would be resigned to the ongoing battle. I think she would be heartened by the smart, fierce people, women especially, who are leading the way and by the young people who are so articulate about the issues. Decades after the civil rights movement began, she would understand that while resistance to change is constant, even more constant is change. Change does happen however frustrating and painful and long the fight. Angie's first foray into writing her opinions for mass consumption (i.e., her high school classmates) today might manifest as mordant morsels on Twitter.

What piece of advice do you have for the little Angies of today—the quiet, the timid, the "different?" In other words, what do you wish someone would have told Angie when she was young?

Miscolta

One of Angie's problems was that she was too often focused on her lack of something in comparison to her peers. It's not until the last few stories that she begins to focus on the things she possesses within herself—her own intelligence or her ability with words, for instance, which she has either not recognized or has undervalued or devalued. There are things that interest or matter to her, but she doesn't trust her own instincts or judgement. There's a world out there full of things to see and do and learn about. Even if you feel that these things are distant from your life at the moment, keep them in your sights, keep moving toward them until they are within reach, and then make the most of them.

Haong

Are you working on any new projects we can be looking forward to?

Miscolta

I'm finishing a novel that is in extension or outgrowth of a story that appeared in *Hola and Goodbye*. The story is called "Strong Girls." It's about these twins who are oversized girls who are big and strong and they are recruited for the boys' wrestling team before they had girls' wrestling teams in schools. I remember when I was trying to sell *Hola and Goodbye*, an editor of a different small press was looking at it and she said, "you know, this story would make an interesting novel," and I hadn't thought of that before, but then I started thinking about how much I liked these characters. These characters are the only characters I created out of my imagination. I didn't draw from somebody I knew or a situation I knew of; they just came to me. The novel I'm working on takes these characters into adulthood. As sisters, as twins, they have a unique relationship, but then they go out into the world and go their separate ways and they each have to face the world as large brown women without the support of each other. The novel deals with body image and sisterhood and self-actualization.

I'm also in the middle of a nonfiction project that consists of essays about identity, race, family, colonization. It's interesting to me to write nonfiction on a personal level because you're writing about people close to you and your family. I've written a couple of essays about each of my parents. They're both dead, which is sort of not fair because they can't see what I write and tell me "that's wrong." I'm also writing essays about immigration and things that are lost, like language. I'm having fun with that because I haven't done a lot of it before.

End of Ecola State Park landslide. Cannon Beach, Oregon. 1963.

Chair, $75 OBO

Erin Pringle

It snowed all morning, and more snow is expected later this afternoon. If snow falls through tomorrow, that would be fine. They have no plans. Last night, they ate out. This morning, they cleaned the house, and now their son's at his father's until tomorrow. It's the weekend, and aside from the detective show her partner's watching at a murmur, the house is quiet. It's quiet outside, too. The sidewalks are shoveled, the stoop swept, and the side street has nothing to do but wait for the plows.

The winter is still new, white and crisp, without slush or ice rutting and sliding beneath boots and tires. Last winter's car-wrecks, school closures, and parking-lot snow berms wait off-stage of memory. Everyone but the homeless are strolling into the winter dream of cozy sweaters and hot chocolate, ski lodges and fireplaces. Christmas lights, ceramic platters passed from mother to daughter. Marshmallows, kindness, cinnamon, family.

Maybe she'll make some cocoa later, in a saucepan like her mother used to do.

For now, she sits by the picture window beyond the TV's reach. A magazine splayed across her lap, words erased by the sun. She feels as lazy as sunlight on a sleeping cat. They don't have any more cats, so they share the neighborhood cat, which her partner won't invite inside. It's a small, purring tabby that presses its skull into the cup of any offered hand.

Her partner finds the cat's trust worrisome.

She finds sturdiness in the cat's trust.

Of all the animals, her sister wanted to be a cat. Blinking slowly. The world slipping in and out of focus. Warm fur, sun-dust on her whiskers. Wouldn't it be so wonderful?

Seems like a lot would depend on the house where you lived as a cat.

It'd be a good house, her sister would say.

What about the family?

It would be a good family.

Seems convenient.

It's a daydream, her sister said.

Then why not be a vegan lion? Or a polar bear napping on a cold waterbed?

It's *my* daydream.

A zebra curled on a hall-rug.

Her sister rolled her eyes.

When they were kids, her sister strangled the family cat at night in their bedroom. The cat's arms would stiffen, its eyes bulge, its lips pull back. Until her sister relaxed her grip.

She never knew if her sister would let go.

She also never told her sister to stop it. Though she would scream it in her head.

Stop!

She'd shut her eyes and try to send her thought into her sister's head.

Stop!

How could her sister want to be a cat? Did she not remember?

She never asked. What if her sister laughed and said, I'm always such a bad guy in all your memories.

Her sister wouldn't say, Bad things were happening to me.

Though they were.

A small gray car turns onto their street and into the frame of the picture window. The car slips, straightens, then trembles as the driver shifts down.

That car.

Are you okay? her partner says.

What?

Her partner picks up the remote and pauses the show. Are you okay?

I'm fine, she says.

You made a sound.

Did I? she says, even though she heard the sound, too.

Yeah.

The gray car is driving slowly. But it can't be her sister's car. *Like* it, but not *it*.

Must have been falling asleep, she says.

Hmm, says her partner in that way.

What?

That's not your napping sound.

How's your show?

Her partner shrugs. You know.

She does. Which is why she sits on the far side of the room from the detective shows her partner loves, and why her partner watches them on nearly silent.

She can still see the gray car at the edge of the picture window. It's a small, boxy car like her sister once drove, years ago. She remembers her sister's blue shorts, bare legs, the triangle of her kneecaps as she pressed the pedals and shifted gears.

Of course, it's not her sister. It's simply the season of snow and holidays, suitcases and family visits—and, thus, unfamiliar vehicles coasting through the neighborhood.

What would have brought her sister here, were that her? Their son's upcoming birthday? Why do sisters visit sisters? To pass out Halloween candy? To take pictures of their nephew's costume?

Her sister loved Halloween.

You're late, she thinks, if that's what brings you.

The gray car wasn't her sister's first or last. Her sister wrecked the first car off a narrow country road on a snowy morning. When she and her mother got there, the car and her sister weren't. Her mother and she drove the curving road. Evidently, someone had beat them to the rescue. Her sister was fine, the car wasn't. Her sister and mother argued about it.

Snow floats through the lace of the tree branches and onto the ground.

It's snowing again, she says.

Mmm, says her partner.

She should put on her coat and start shoveling. She swept the porch stairs a little after she woke up. Once she's in her winter coat and plugged into headphones, she could stay out the rest of the day. The rhythm of that work is easy to disappear into.

A woman screams.

Jesus, she says, turning.

Sorry, says her partner and picks up the remote. The green volume grid appears on the screen, losing bars.

Here's the gray car again. It's coming from the other direction now, back down the hill. Lost, maybe. She shouldn't feel so unnerved.

The snow falls.

She can't make out the driver's face, but the driver's wearing a green winter hat like their father did. Their mother's winter hat was variegated shades of purple. When she and her sister were kids, anyway. Now, her mother wears store-bought hats in nondescript fleece. Grays and gray-blues. Most of her memories take place in childhood. After that, they blur, they float, they stick or sink.

What color was her sister's winter hat?

Not green.

She starts dressing hats on the memory of her sister like a paper doll's ghost.

Orange? No.

Yellow? Nope.

Their father's hat had a matching green pom-pom. Their grandmother had crocheted it. She remembers him opening the gift, and Mom wishing he loved it. He wound up wearing it to bed on winter nights because their mother kept the house thermostat down to beat last month's utility bill. When the cancer came, he wore it through spring and summer.

Now she has the green hat, which their son wore the other day, though he's only five. It's the elasticity of the crochet, she guesses. This was your grandfather's hat, she told him.

What are you thinking? her partner says.

About my dad's hat.

Is today an anniversary? Her partner keeps track of all the death anniversaries in her phone calendar. She's seen them listed there. Her dad's death. Her sister's. Her dad's birthday. Her sister's.

No, I was just thinking about it.

What do you think about it?

I don't know.

Should you go for a run?

I'm fine.

You like to run in the snow, says her partner.

I probably will tonight.

Good.

She loves night runs during snowfall, the quiet, being the only one out, how the sky rises into darker and darker grays above the streetlights that glow like smoke. And the chimneys, too, lit for the first time of the season.

Did her sister even wear hats? She had so much hair. Long, curly hair that defied gravity and the rules about how much space a polite girl should inhabit. A hat on her sister would have been like a corset.

Where did her sister even keep her winter hats once she moved out? In their childhood home, they were piled on the floor of the front hall closet.

She tries to remember closets in her sister's trailers. She was still in grade school when her sister moved out. That was lonely and awful. But her sister let her sleep over most weekends and would come get her and drive her through town to the light-fixture factory near that first trailer, the pink and white one. Her sister's next trailer was gray and out in the country, off an unmarked road surrounded by cornfields and bean fields. It had a black mailbox, a gray cat named Smokey Joe, and at some point, her sister got a dog named Dog.

She remembers the kitchen cabinets, their fake wood veneer. She remembers her sister reporting that she'd found dead mice under the sink. Their father thought it was funny. She felt bad for her sister. How did her sister seem?

It doesn't matter now.

Grossed out, probably.

Go shovel the snow. Shovel both sidewalks, the whole block. You'll feel better. You'll get your head out of there.

The gray car is back, and it's pulling over.

It parks in front of their house.

The driver hunches over the steering wheel, looking up the small hill to their house. It's hard to read their house number where it's screwed on the porch post. She keeps meaning to paint the numbers with bright colors.

Probably the neighbors ordered delivery. Because of the snow. Because it's the weekend. Any minute, Jim will come out of his house to take a bag from the driver. Fresh fries, maybe. Pasta. A container of miniature cinnamon rolls. Jim will see her in the window, wave. She'll wave back. He'll turn back to the house, she'll lower her hands to the arm rests, and the driver who is not her sister will drive away.

The gray car is still there.

Could be a salesman.

A signature collector.

The piano tuner.

Stop it. Go shovel in the back yard. Take a bath. Boil hot water for tea. Find a book to read. Toast a bagel. Walk laps around the house dining table like your grandfather used to.

The driver door swings open. The driver gets out, but now leans into the backseat.

Are you expecting anyone? she says to her partner.

Her partner pauses the TV. What's that?

A package or a visitor or something?

Her partner frowns. Why?

No reason.

Why?

Oh, there's a car just pulled up.

I'm not. Are you?

Nope.

Okay.

It's a gray car. Like my sister drove.

Her partner looks at her like this every time her sister comes up. Like a large, stained glass chandelier is about to snap from the ceiling, but she doesn't know whether to catch it or step aside.

I mean, it's not *her* car. It's just *like* her car. A car like she drove when I was little. It's whatever. It's nothing.

It's not nothing.

She shrugs. It's whatever. Just wondered if you were expecting anybody. Probably it's a delivery for the neighbors. Flowers, maybe.

Maybe.

Might be our future neighbors.

Our luck.

We'd have to move.

Her partner looks at her steadily.

Joke. Just joking.

But could she bear to see that car every day? She'd have to. Just like her mother somehow bore seeing Dad's van around town after he died and someone bought it. Life is bearing it. That's what she's learned. Put that on a bumper sticker.

Chances are good it's the next neighbor. The house next door is a rental with revolving neighbors. Nobody stays long before moving out or being arrested. How does the landlord consistently find people who never stay? It's the only house in the neighborhood like it, but there you go. She thinks of it as a trick house. From the curb, it looks like all the others. Split-level, front and back yards. Trees. Until you look closer. Paint fissuring. Old wasp nests between the guttering and overhang. Dead trees in the backyard. She's decided the tenants don't see all that because the surrounding houses aren't falling apart, just as you'd never know that people disappear if you didn't know the people disappearing.

Your sister's been on your mind a lot lately, her therapist will say at the next session.

She's always on my mind.

The therapist will wait for silence to fill the office.

Yeah, she'll admit. A lot lately.

Why right now?

I don't know, but did I tell you about the other day at the coffee shop? This connects. Listen, a lady walked in and stopped. There's a woman already there, having coffee, reading the paper or something.

The lady who just came in says to her, You look like my sister.

Oh? says the other woman.

Yes. The lady keeps staring at her. Then realizes it. Sorry, she says. I just . . . I'm sorry. My sister's been dead for four years, and . . .

It's okay.

It's just . . . it's so good to see you.

The therapist said, What did you think about it?

I understood it.

You'd like to see your sister again.

Of course. Yes. Absolutely.

And here we are this snowy day, and there's her sister's ghost letting down the back seats of a car she drove thirty years ago.

If her sister's ghost comes up to the house, should she ask for some kind of ID? If you don't mind, I need to see your knee. There should be a scar where my sister busted her knee on a rock when she was five or six.

Does a ghost retain every scar? Her sister's scars became more visible after her death.

She and her mother cataloged them.

Did you know about . . . ?

Yes, but did you know about the time when . . . ?

I didn't.

I've started to wonder if . . .

If that is her sister's ghost, this is exactly what she'll do. She'll get a knife from the kitchen and cut her sister's death off of her as one cuts scales from a fish, shadows from feet, memories from time.

So what's left is just her sister.

That's what she probably misses most. Having a sister without a death.

Would the ghost of her sister even recognize the sister she was talking about?

Perhaps when meeting your own ghost there's a space of time reserved to tell your ghost the stories of yourself.

Here we are, your ghost will say.

Looks like it.

You sit across from each other at a table, waiting for the other to speak.

I thought you didn't believe in ghosts, your ghost will say.

Suppose I'll have to believe in my own, you say.

In this way, the ghost will say, perhaps reading aloud from a manual, death is not so different from life.

What stories of her life would she tell the ghost? How does a ghost interpret the life it supposedly extends from?

When she and her partner fell in love, she felt relieved never to have to tell her life to anyone again.

The driver straightens, stretches her arms over her head, then shuts the door and looks up at the house. She wears large tortoiseshell sunglasses.

Nope.

But she is. Look.

Nope.

Memory of sitting in a wind-up swing, and her sister says, I'll be right back and runs up the stairs, and when her sister returns, she sets those sunglasses on her. The sunglasses darken her sight.

Her sister laughed. Someone took a picture. How happy her sister was. Was she?

Yes, she was happy. She was. Her death wasn't there, way back then.

And if it was?

Could it have been?

The driver shades her face with a mitten. The mittens are colorful and thickly crocheted. They're warmer than gloves, her sister said, because your fingers are allowed to touch.

The gray car was always cold. Maybe the heater was broken. It was always the radio or the heater.

The driver steps onto the sidewalk and approaches the stairs. She wears a plaid winter coat and a striped scarf. Her mitten slides along the railing in the way a stranger's would, but also in that unsure way her sister came down the stairway on prom night, hand on the railing, in that electric blue dress with black netting. Her sister's prom date waited in the living room. Stewart? Steven? S-Something.

Electric, the prom date said.

Her sister smiled, trying to keep her lips over her braces.

Their mother handed her sister the plastic corsage container from the fridge. Her sister took out the blue carnation and matching wrist corsage.

Several years later, it was her turn to come down the stairs in a prom dress, her high heels catching on the carpeting while her college-age sister watched from the kitchen with their parents and their father's cancer.

Beautiful, her sister said.

But am I electric? she said.

What?

The driver in the tortoiseshell sunglasses has reached the top stair and now walks to the porch stairs. Is that how her sister walked? She should recognize her sister's walk.

Stop it.

It's not her.

But if you keep thinking like this, you'll have to tell your therapist, and you don't want another session about your sister.

At least for a while.

What if her partner hired someone to act like her sister? She read an article about Japan or somewhere where actors are hired to be ordinary. One woman has an actor for her child's father, and the child doesn't know her real father left years ago. The actor is a good father.

Even if the child wondered, how could the child ever ask?

Are actresses ever hired to resume the lives of dead women?

Is that why so many dead women are never found?

And what about the retirement community in that European village, built for dementia patients who have no idea their maids are nurses.

How many dark worlds exist in order for this one to roll along, as though by an understandable gravity?

There's the knock at the door.

Did you hear that? her partner says.

Someone's here.

I didn't know we were expecting anyone.

It's the gray car, she says.

Oh?

I'll get it, she says. Her legs have already unfolded, and she stands. She can feel the hole in her sock, the ridges. She feels very aware of the chair, her body, the person waiting a door away. And she also feels none of it. A hollowing.

Perhaps I've had a heart attack, and I'm dying. This is dying. She waits to see her partner hurry over, drop to her knees, press her cheek to her chest and heart.

Instead, her partner pulls the blanket up to her armpits and frowns at the TV.

So. Not dying. Just alive in that dying way, I guess.

She watches herself walk across the room.

When she opens the door, their son will be standing there. Why'd you lock it? he'll say, then push past her, saying he forgot his swim shorts for the YMCA.

When she opens the door, two teenage girls will stand there with a clipboard and say, Climate Change.

She'll open the door to a traveling salesman holding a vacuum cleaner.

We don't have carpeting, she'll say.

Ah! I have just the thing, he'll say, and snap open a briefcase. From it, he'll lift a cat with bulging eyes and stiffened arms.

Stop it.

She'll open the door to her dead sister with her stiffened arms.

Enough.

She'll open the door to a neighbor a few streets away. Their mail came to her house. That's mundane enough to be the most likely.

She opens the door to her sister.

The doormat reads WELCOME.

She and her sister look at each other. Her sister smiles and pushes back the sunglasses. There is her sister's whole face in the center of all that hair. Her sister. Right there.

Hi, says her sister.

Seeing her sister's face is different from imagining her sister's face.

I'm here about the chair, says her sister.

I hope this isn't a bad time, her sister says.

Her sister examines her face.

The chair?

Yes, the reading chair that you're selling. Maybe this isn't the right address. Her sister pulls off her mitten and reaches into her coat pocket. She takes out a crumpled tissue and stuffs it back in. She reaches into her back pocket and takes out a piece of paper. It's folded in fours and the fold lines look new.

2418, says her sister, reading off the paper. They both glance at the metal 2-4-1-8 screwed vertically down the porch post.

Liberty? says her sister.

Yes. Liberty Avenue.

Her sister hands her the paper.

She doesn't want to take it.

But she does. She feels the paper fold back on itself but doesn't look at it. She doesn't want to see that note even if she's read it before. Why did her sister write one? Out of politeness? Out of respect for the genre of suicide? Because that's just what people do, no differently than people write thank-you notes?

Her sister's note was more white space than handwriting—so much whiteness that now she dreams of it falling around her like snowfall after extinction, burying cars and people with their screams.

Though she thinks when the world does end, people will be calm about it. Drinking coffee and doing the crossword. Wondering if they need rice or already have some in the pantry.

See? her sister says and points at the paper.

As though turning a knob jutting from her ear, she lets her head tilt down, taking her eyes with it.

Between the folded lines is not her sister's handwriting. It's a picture of her reading chair. The one behind her. The one she was just sitting in with the blue velvet pillow and cat scratches.

The only difference is that the chair floats in white space instead of beside a wall half-covered by a bookcase.

My chair, she says.

Oh, good, her sister says. So you haven't sold it yet?

She shakes her head.

Excellent, says her sister or her sister's ghost. It doesn't matter which now.

Her sister says, I should have called, but then I wound up in the neighborhood. Maybe they're home, I thought. So. Sometimes whims pan out, I thought.

Not always, she says.

Her sister shrugs. Here you are.

Here you are, she says.

Of course her sister would drop in without calling, because her sister died before cell phones, before people knew to text ahead.

People killed themselves for different reasons. Or different causes for the same feelings. She has thought of her sister's death like a craving, but was it one that would have weakened, or was it one that strengthened?

She thought her sister knew, but clearly her sister doesn't know about her death. How could she, in a warm coat and with snowflakes in her hair?

One time her sister said, If I came back as anything, it would be as a cat. The neighborhood tabby is not her sister after all.

She returns the paper to the driver of the gray car who is coincidentally a lot like her dead sister. Coincidences, you know they do happen. Or feel like they happen.

You should come in, she says. It's cold out there. She wants to say, You look good, but she doesn't want to make the woman feel awkward or uncomfortable. Who says that to someone who's come to buy used furniture?

Her sister-who-can't-be-her-sister smiles and slips the paper into her coat pocket. The coat looks nice on her, wherever she got it. Put together. That's how their mother would describe her. The jeans her sister's wearing don't have grass on the knees, as the autopsy described.

Turns out her sister didn't die, after all.

So, where's the burst of confetti? The news cameras? The three-story cake?

I'll wait, she thinks.

But of course, she won't. Instead, she opens the door and steps to the side, nearly falling over her son's snow boots, so her sister can walk off the porch and into the house. She glances down at her sister's footprints coming up the snow on the path she swept from here to the stairs. The gray car is still down at the curb.

Hello, she hears her partner saying.

Hello, she hears her sister say.

Why did you keep thinking of the stranger as your sister? she imagines her therapist saying.

She follows her sister inside, pulling the door shut behind her.

There's snow on the floor where her sister stands. Her sister crouches and unties her snow boots. They're nice boots, expensive like all the other mothers wear at the preschool where her son goes. Her sister never visited her in the Northwest, never saw this house, never addressed a letter to here, never met her partner, never even learned she was gay. That came after. Their mother got to learn that by herself, over the phone.

So, there you go, she said.

Her mother didn't answer.

Mom, I know you're still there.

I am.

Well . . . ?

I don't know. I don't know what to say. What should I say? What would your father have said?

Only their mother would say exactly the same words to her about being gay as she would about her sister's suicide. I just don't understand it, their mother said as they drove to the funeral. What would your father say?

He wouldn't believe it, her mother said. Do you believe it?

The cornfields passed from windshield to side windows to the rearview mirror, field after field moving from front to back, powerline after powerline, until she started thinking the car must be sitting still while the world did the moving, the world was what pulled the road like a crumpled ribbon out from under them, the world spun the fields, tossed the clouds, took her sister's breath away and locked it in a treasure box that no she and her mother had to bury.

Did you hear what I said? her mother would have said usually, but instead she'd slipped into one of the fogs they both fell into since then.

I used to help her memorize lines.

That's what you're thinking? her mother said. Her mother had clear ideas about what to think about when grieving. And she never did it right.

She'd sat on her sister's bedroom carpet, holding another play script while her sister sat in front of her on the dresser, eating an ice-cream sandwich while waiting for the cue for her next line.

That's you, she'd say.

Not yet.

It is.

Doesn't so and so have to say such and such first?

No.

Are you sure?

I'm the one with the script, aren't I?

Fine. What's my line?

She'd read it, and then her sister would hop off the dresser and repeat it, slowing it down, pausing, with a tilt of her head or a flourish of her hand.

When her sister died, she kept thinking, This was not in the script.

She didn't expect to think that, didn't expect her sister to die, so how did her mother expect her to guess what her father would have said about her sister's death or her own gayness?

This was not in the script.

What script?

You know. The script. The *script*.

There isn't a script.

I was told there was a script.

Who told you about a script?

I don't know. I have a feeling. I just had a feeling.

It has been both long and not long since her sister died, and it always will be like that. Maybe that's why her sister doesn't recognize her. She imagines the world looked very different to her sister before the end. And wouldn't she have been included in that view of the world her sister held?

Lately, she has started seeing her sister around town.

What's that like? said her therapist.

Like when her bike was stolen from her yard years ago in a different city and state, but still, she sometimes sees a bike like that one—for a second. It never is her bike or her sister. But for the moment that it is, it's nice. Really nice.

Inside the house, her partner sits in front of the TV, and her sister stands by the tray where they set their snowy boots. The TV is paused. Two investigators sit in a tavern over a pint and clues to who murdered this episode's dead woman.

Her partner looks from her to her sister, then back.

Probably she should just introduce them. Get it over with. This is . . .

Oh! says her sister, pulling her other foot out of her boot. How rude of me. Her sister laughs. Sorry. I'm Faye.

Faye, her partner says.

It's Faye, she says. Gray car.

Her partner's eyes widen.

That's me, says her sister Faye, then gives a little wave. Then laughs. And her sister's laugh blooms from that one. Evidently, she didn't do well folding them into one, packing it away with the family videos her mother sent her from time to time. But that she never played.

She leans against the door. She can feel it against her shoulder blades.

Faye's a lovely name, says her partner.

She can tell that her partner's not having the same experience that she is. Her partner never heard her sister laugh.

I'm here about the chair, says Faye.

The chair? says her partner, holding the blanket under her armpits.

My reading chair that's for sale.

I didn't know you were selling it.

Didn't you?

Her partner slowly shakes her head, trying to catch up.

Would you like to sit in it, Faye?

Faye nods, then smiles. Those dimples.

She never imagined ghosts would smile so much.

I knew I shouldn't have come in on you like this, Faye says. Who does that? That's what my sister would say.

Your sister?

Faye nods and steps past her to the chair. She stands in front of it, admiring. I love it, she says.

Are you buying the chair for your sister?

Oh, no. Faye stops smiling. She would have loved it, though. Can I try it?

Go ahead.

Faye turns and sits, then leans back, her arms on the armrests. The chair creaks. It's warm, Faye says.

I was just sitting there, she says.

Faye looks out the window. How long have you had it?

I bought it after my sister died, she says.

Oh, Faye says, and turns to look at her.

It was a while ago.

Still, says Faye. I can't imagine.

Can't you?

I'm going to make some popcorn, her partner says and stands up.

Popcorn.

That's right, says her partner. Faye, would you like to stay and watch a show with us? That way you can really know if you like the chair. I've wished I could do something like that when I've been furniture shopping.

Really? Faye says.

We don't have plans, says her partner. Do you like mysteries?

I was going to shovel, she says.

It's still snowing.

Better to stay ahead of it.

Do you like mysteries, Faye?

Not really, Faye says.

She laughs. Faye and her partner look at her.

Can you help me in the kitchen? her partner says and starts toward it.

She starts to follow. But what if when she leaves the room, Faye disappears? Or, what if Faye starts to remember that she's dead? Once she remembers, will she want to leave? Will she feel embarrassed? Even if she did end her life, she can imagine her sister being embarrassed at being found out. As though she didn't hide the evidence well enough. Like when she'd sneak snacks from the kitchen and their mother would find the plates gathering ants under her sister's bed.

I just don't understand, their mother would say.

I was hungry.

But why hide it?

Her sister would shrug.

Her partner leans against the kitchen sink. So, she says.

I don't think she knows.

Your sister.

That's right.

Your sister wants to buy your reading chair.

Do you think I should just give it to her?

Her partner rubs her eyes and slowly shakes her head.

She steps back to see into the living room. Faye is still in the chair. Faye must see her in the reflection of the window because she turns and gives a little wave. It's really snowing, she says.

You could get snowed in.

Then you'll never get rid of me, says Faye.

That's a good one.

We'll have to share the chair.

Take turns.

Make a schedule. You take it on the weekends. I'll take it through the week.

Faye laughs.

She ducks back into the kitchen. My sister says it's really snowing, she says to her partner. And when she hears herself, she remembers saying it all the time.

My sister says you can sit on a tack.

My sister says the Mona Lisa feels uncomfortable.

My sister says sex isn't that at all, and she's in fourth grade so she should know.

My sister says frogs don't realize they're in boiling water if it starts cold and warms up over time.

My sister says she'll be over for Christmas in the afternoon because her boyfriend's family has some kind of morning tradition. I don't know.

My sister named her dog Dog.

My sister says don't make the mistake she did majoring in literature.

My sister says nothing, I haven't heard from her since I called and she said she felt so heavy.

My sister says she's feeling better. This new medication should help.

My sister wants to know what she was like before the medication. She doesn't believe she could have been *that* bad. She just wants to remember that self.

In the kitchen, her partner takes her in her arms.

They stand there like that a while. Her partner is warm and solid and safe. Focus on that, she thinks. The soft nubby yarn of her sweater. The ridge of her shoulder. The sweet smell of yesterday's gel still in her hair. Her tender cheek.

We're going to watch a mystery show, her partner says.

And eat popcorn.

With your sister.

With Faye.

That's right. That's fine.

It's not usual, she says.

No, says her partner.

But it's fine. It has to be, right?

That's right.

And it has to be okay that this Faye doesn't recognize me.

Sure.

It's okay if this Faye doesn't know she's a ghost.

She is who she is.

Whoever that is.

Yes.

Ghost or not. We don't know what ghosts don't know. And it might be nice to get to know this Faye.

This Faye.

This Faye.

Maybe this Faye won't. . .

They look at each other.

Should I call my mom?

Would she believe you?

She'd want to know.

Yes. Her partner nods and continues to hold her.

She rubs her forehead. She's glad not to be let go of. How did they let go of Faye? How did she get so far away before anyone noticed? Or was she not far away? Surely there were footprints.

Then they let go, and she focuses on cutting open the popcorn bag.

I am making popcorn for my dead sister, she thinks. No, for my sister.

For Faye who bent every summer over handfuls of jacks she scattered across the sidewalk.

Faye crouched in a school hallway during a tornado drill.

Faye coming down the stairs in that prom dress. Electric.

Faye pushing down her hair, grimacing in the bathroom mirror.

Faye saying kissing will get better, you'll see. It's just your first time.

Faye on the ground as policemen walk around her.

And now Faye sits in their living room watching the snow fall.

The popcorn starts hammering against the bag.

I've always wanted to meet her, says her partner.

And I've wanted to know how she's doing.

Yes.

So this is good.

Absolutely good.

Can I invite her to dinner?

Sure. You could offer to deliver the chair to her house.

I don't think it will fit in her car, even with the seats down.

It fits in yours. Then you can see where she calls home.

I love you.

And I love you.

The popcorn stops. She opens the microwave and takes out the bag. CAUTION, it says, OIL CAN BURN.

Her partner takes a bowl from the cabinet.

Should we have more than one bowl?

Probably.

When she carries the popcorn into the living room, Faye's still in the chair but now curled up sideways. Her eyes are closed, but she's breathing. She watches the lift of her shoulders to be sure. She's napping.

It's still snowing.

She carefully sets the bowls on the coffee table. Then takes the wool throw off the back of the couch, and gently unfolds it across her sister's body. She tucks it around her shoulders and between her back and the cushion. It's not the best napping chair, but it will work.

She kneels in front of the chair and rests her cheek on Faye's lap. Faye is warm and so real. She can see the fine hairs on her cheek and where her eyelashes meet. Outside, a crumble of snow falls from the tree and into the snow that passed through. The snow should fall awhile longer.

Clouds Taken for Mountains

Nicholas Bradley

For one reason
or another

I hadn't flown
for months, the habit

of airports having
escaped me,

the familiar
terminal hassles –

the scans and checks –
having given way

to familial
excursions, brief

trips by car
that the baby

would endure,
and on my first night

away, as the sun
set on my flight

to Santa Ana,
to a desert respite

from drizzle,
rendezvous with friends

in creosote
country, he went

to bed as usual,
I imagined,

and said so long
(in his mother's

voice) to his books
and mobile, bears

and rabbits, and cried
till sleep relieved him

at five past seven,
and I was left

alone with a full
moon pink outside

the continental
window, craters

and spires beneath
the cloudland drifting

under the portside
wing, my purpose now

to learn how to leave
and return without

disquiet or heartbreak,
to let him be

and to be constant,
even in mid-air,

when one thing
looks like another.

Lightning storm over Bearhead Mountain.
Snoqualmie National Forest, Washington. 1938.

A Certain Brightness

Soramimi Hanarejima

1.

Even a week after swapping, I didn't mind that you wouldn't give mine back to me. I still liked having your reflection—having her company in the bathroom, seeing my delight curling her lips, reminded by her posture to keep my back straight. Those gleaming eyes you appeared to see with so clearly, sensitive to things in their corners, looking right back at me—freckles below like a hermit thrush's speckled chest. A little taller than me, she seemed just slightly ahead of me in growing up, encouraging me to catch up, showing me something of what I could soon become. I wanted to see more of that and more… just more. I stood in front of the mirror for a long time before taking a shower—and afterwards too, when she was wet with the water on my body. Maybe you did the same thing.

I wanted to ask my mom if she had ever traded reflections when she was a child, but I worried that just mentioning this might upset her the way some benign things unexpectedly did.

2.

Besides this unease about how my mom would react, nothing about the swap really bothered me. There were just minor inconveniences, like not being able to tell if I had combed my hair properly in the mornings, and having to be careful around mirrors in places with other people to avoid unnecessary attention. So at school, I'd only use the bathroom when I was pretty sure it would be empty, and if someone came in, I waited in a stall until they were gone, then washed my hands as quickly as I could.

3.

I wanted to tell your reflection that she didn't have to copy all my movements because mimicry didn't matter to me. But I was afraid that when we switched back—whenever that was going to be—she would be out of practice and wouldn't imitate you correctly.

Instead, I told her the things I wanted to tell you: how one day we would go on adventures together, rafting down raging rivers and slashing our way through jungles to find ancient ruins; how you could count on me to write your biography after you became famous; how I had once seen my mom hurl the toaster against the kitchen floor, then laugh, then cry a little, and then at breakfast, she acted like nothing had happened—how I never saw the toaster again.

I thought your reflection might somehow tell you these things later—maybe in dreams, when she could become anything, like a talking leopard or a long-lost twin.

4.

In her own way, she told me things too. Some that I'd find out more about later, like your very short haircut, which I then saw at school the next day. And some things that I would never find out about, like all the crying you must have done to make your reflection's eyes red and puffy.

5.

Hoping that she might tell me more, I made it a point to look as closely as I could at your reflection's eyes, searching for clues to your feelings in there—the only part of her unchanged by my actions. But no matter how deeply I peered into her eyes, I didn't see anything. Maybe a glimmer of joy or twinkle of delight or smoldering of anger. Probably my imagination making something of the sunlight through the bathroom window. Because would I even recognize emotion if I saw it in your eyes? Were they even there?

I asked my mom if it was in fact possible to read emotions in a person's eyes.

"Sometimes," Mom answered. "There's a certain brightness you can see."

So of course, I began studying your eyes for that brightness.

6.

What I liked most about having your reflection was seeing her in the bathroom mirror at night. She reminded me that in the vast, quiet darkness outside, you were close by—on the other side of town, on the other side of the night when you'd be back in the same classroom as me. Your reflection also reminded me that we could be connected in other ways besides the usual ones of talking and activities, like playing badminton or making pizza.

This often got me excited that we could be connected in more ways when we were older, too old to switch reflections anymore; when we would grow other parts of ourselves—new tastes, complex abilities and stronger qualities, including the ones our teachers spoke highly of: patience, compassion, resolve. The kind of things that I couldn't see in your reflection but that she reminded me of, like the way you'd pay attention to Ms. Darqli reading poetry and birds singing in the woods by closing your eyes to listen carefully.

7.

I also liked the flights of fantasy your reflection would suddenly launch me into. The first one that really got my attention was on that sunny afternoon I rode my bicycle too close to a neighbor's rose bush and scratched up my leg. As soon as I got home, I went straight to the bathroom, to get the antiseptic ointment from the medicine cabinet above the sink. When I opened the medicine cabinet, swinging its mirrored door over to the left, your reflection pivoted out to the side with it, seeming to reveal the memories neatly arranged within you, right behind your sharp eyes and round cheeks. Like all the bottles and tubes on the little shelves held not pills and lotions but moments, pieces of the past tucked away for later—or never. Like I could open these containers and get glimpses of who you were before you moved here and other times you never told me about.

Staring at tubes of creams and bottles of tinctures inside the medicine cabinet, I forgot all about those rose-thorn scratches on my right shin, becoming lost in thoughts about what memories I'd put in your mind if I could reach in there: a mouthful of hazelnut ice cream from the creamery down the street from my grandparents' place, the sea lion show you missed when you were sick the day of the aquarium field trip, my favorite lullaby, the silhouette of a great-horned owl in a eucalyptus tree stretching its body out to hoot.

8.

Then there was the Saturday night you slept over, when we were brushing our teeth together in the bathroom. Our reflections were in the same mirror for the first time since we had swapped. Diagonally across from me, mine was doing everything you were—brushing, spitting, rinsing—and in front of me, yours was doing everything I was. It was as though we were seeing another world where we were each living the other's life. The longer I looked, the more I was convinced that our world and theirs could flip at any moment, then tomorrow I would go home to your parents. But of course, nothing happened. We finished brushing our teeth and went back to my room. After playing glow-in-the-dark dominos, we got into bed.

I switched on the planetarium to fill the ceiling with specs of light, and a moment later, you asked, "Does anyone else know?"

"No," I answered. Who was there to tell?

"I think my mom is getting suspicious," you said.

"Should we switch back?"

"Only if she says something."

She never did. Or if she did, you never told me. Either way, I was relieved when the next school week ended without any mention of this.

9.

And ended instead with an afternoon at your house and you showing me a trick I hadn't thought to try.

"Check this out," you said, after bringing me into your parents' bathroom.

You angled your mother's makeup mirror at my reflection in the mirror above the sink. The arrangement created a little tunnel of reflected mirrors, and repeating throughout it was the endless alternation of my face and yours.

"Because the reflection of your reflection is my reflection," you explained.

Which made immediate sense. If a mirror reflected you to me, then it should reflect my reflection to your reflection. Despite the clear logic of it, I remained astonished by the ceaseless sequence of our staggered images.

10.

That Sunday, I went on one of those long drives in the country that Mom needed in order to "mentally cleanse." Whenever the direction of the late-morning sunlight was right, I stared at your reflection on the passenger-side window, faint against hills, fields, woods or sky. Mom always kept her eyes on the road, so I didn't have to worry that she'd notice. I wondered how your reflection felt as sunlight streamed through her and the world rushed by behind her. Could she see what was on both sides of the window at once?

11.

The blur of a farm stand streaked by, and I began to imagine what it would be like to always have her company like this during long drives and train rides. I pictured myself old enough to drive, making my way down a country highway, pulling over and stepping out to buy strawberries from a farm stand, seeing your reflection in the car window when I close the door, walking away as though I'm leaving her to wait in the car, the way Mom sometimes did with me.

This would be after you disappear, never to be heard from again—whisked away by wizards to fight a war in the magical kingdom you had always been the secret heir to. Leaving me here with your reflection as she gradually reveals how the years change your appearance. Or how they don't because time passes differently between our two worlds. As I age, your reflection stays young, always a reminder of our childhood days together—except during the couple weeks I see a fox in the mirror because you need to keep yourself disguised while making your way through enchanted woods.

12.

Or you don't disappear, but we wait too long to switch back, and your reflection becomes fully attached to me. Then, would there be days when I don't want to look in any mirror, keep my gaze away from all reflective surfaces? Maybe after some argument or a major decision we disagree on. And I finally find out how seeing your reflection can hurt just as much as—or more than—it can comfort and delight.

13.

I turned to Mom and wondered how much hurt and how much delight I had brought her so far. There seemed no way to really tell. Over the years, so many things had happened, and sometimes, I couldn't tell how Mom felt about those things. Other times, one of us would forget how something had felt or that it had even happened. Usually I would be the one who forgot. Mom would often describe a place or event, then ask, "Remember that?" and I couldn't.

But I could say for myself with certainty that Mom had made me happy more than she had ever made me sad or angry.

14.

And this brought to mind the concept of ratios, which we had started learning and you were good at, making bold declarations like "Two to one!" after a classmate had tentatively offered "Ten to five."

As Mom's car continued to zip down the road, there seemed now some similarity between how math and the heart compared things. They both dealt in relative amounts and proportions. Not always but in meaningful ways.

Like right here, the calm of Mom's steady focus on driving far outweighed the lingering unease about how she'd react to me having your reflection. And that comparison led me to decide that I would make the ratio of delight to hurt as high as I could for the people who mattered most to me. Make its fraction form infinite, if I could—a divide by zero situation, at least on some days.

15.

"You're missing the scenery," Mom said, eyes still aimed straight ahead. "Is the sun too hot on your side? You can turn up the air conditioning if you want."

"No, I'm fine," I answered.

"OK. Then why don't you tell me what's out there, outside my field of view," she said.

So, with hurried words trying to keep pace with everything going by, I described the grazing cows, the red tractor and stand of trees, the perched shrike, the wire fences and bales of rolled up hay—the myriad things on the other side of your reflection, appearing as though they were all in her imagination. Sunshine was on everything, my face aglow with a brightness that I hoped you could see, that seemed to make both of us the narrators of this unspooling landscape.

Shiras Moose, Hoodoo Lake, Lolo National Forest.
Selway Wilderness area, Idaho. 1925.

The Ballad of Aunt Lottie

Rena Priest

Will and I are 16. Will drives, I don't. Our dad gives Will the keys and sends us to the store for spray paint for his buoys. At the hardware store a pimply-faced kid behind the paint counter slams his clipboard down. We look up in surprise and the boy says to the other boy, "You have to watch the Indians. They'll steal anything."

We leave without buying what we need and now our father will have to spend more gas money going back and forth on the long ride from the reservation to town. Later that night I watch an episode of *48 Hours* about a white man who steals women from their families and keeps them in a bunker underground until he steals their lives. I fall asleep and in my dream I am watching white men in boats rounding up killer whales in a cove, taking the babies from their keening mothers. The dream changes and Will and I are on the city bus when we run into Lottie. This dream is a memory. I am happy to see Aunt Lottie again. She disappeared and nobody could ever get the police to look for her.

She used to come over as often as once a week. We called her Rez Santa because she would arrive bearing trash bags full of the latest fashions; everything that cost too much at the mall. She loved it when she saw that you liked something she'd picked out for you. She even swiped things on order. Taking a trip? She'd swipe you some fancy luggage.

Throwing a party? She'd steal you a prime rib roast with all the fixins. She'd committed to memory the shoe, pant, shirt, and dress size of all her family and friends. She knew everyone's style and kept them in mind when she gathered. "Gathering." That's what she called it, and that's how she approached it, just like a pre-contact Indian strolling through the forest taking what she needed.

The malls have security guards to protect the goods, but the only thing watching over nature is a person's awareness of how an ecosystem works. Take too much and there won't be enough next time. Malls have a type of artificial ecosystem, too. She learned its ways in order to operate. Just like in the old days when a hunter fasted and bathed in mountain streams to smell like the landscape, she only wore the classiest clothes and made it so everything about her seemed expensive, even the way she smelled. Knowing how to look like she belonged was how she kept the racket going.

In the dream, on the bus, Aunt Lottie is decked out in a beautiful white wool suit.

"Why you riding the bus?" Will asks.

"Gotta go see about a car," she says, and winks.

We suspect that she meant *Gotta go steal a car.*

"Hey Lottie? How come you steal all the time? Don't you feel bad for stealing from the shops?" I ask.

Will kicks my ankle. But Aunt Lottie smiles and says, "Aw Niecey someday you'll understand. It goes back to the treaty. They made a promise in that treaty that we would be allowed to harvest in our usual and accustomed fishing, hunting, and harvesting grounds. But look, they've paved it all over and made it private property and now there's nothing there to harvest but clothes and jewelry and fine home furnishings. You see?" She gestured out the window of the bus, then, after enough concrete had passed to make her point, she went on. "No more temxw, no more kelsip, no more alile or saski in the springtime. Have a pop tart, kid.

"Let me tell you something, our U&A—that's what we call our usual and accustomed harvesting grounds—our U&A ran all the way from the

Columbia River, up into the Frasier Valley. Vancouver, Washington, to Vancouver, B.C. I suppose I don't need to tell you that the Columbia River and British Columbia are both named for that dirtbag Columbus, and both Vancouvers are named for that other scum, Captain Vancouver. You learn about the 'Explorers' yet?"

I shake my head yes.

"Explorers, my ass! Greedy men with ships is all they were. Don't believe everything those teachers say. I bet you think they know it all. Do you think they know it all?"

I shake my head no.

"Good. Anyway, the xwenitems paved the whole thing over, so now this is how I hunt and gather. If they ain't going to give us an education like they promised in the treaty, and if we can't get decent, honest jobs because those are only for educated whites, then we got to make our own way. You understand? There's a difference you know, between being smart and being educated." She eyes me to make sure I am following.

"Do you know what the principal told the teachers at school? He said, 'Don't bother with the Indian kids 'cause they can't learn.' And let me tell you, those teachers sure didn't bother. And you know what? To hell with 'em! Who says we can't learn? Those fools at Sears still haven't learned that chaining up the binoculars is just a show for the dummies, when they sell wire-snippers two aisles over. Who can't learn, babe?"

We laugh together and then she says sternly, "Not to say that what I do is okay, and don't you two ever do it. I know it's wrong, and I know God is gonna punish me. But I help people, too." She pulls the cord for the next stop.

"How else is some broke-ass little Indian kids going to be able to wear some fancy pants and feel good about themself when the whites go around rubbing our faces in what we don't have? The haves and the have-nots. Someday you'll see." She looked away and continued. "Yeah, I'm a thief, but look at it another way, who's the thief? They got the whole continent in exchange for some smallpox infected blankets."

She pauses.

"You think about what I'm telling you. They tried to wipe us out completely, but here we are, so we won! You're a smart kid," she says, "You can learn. I expect you to work hard and get an education so you can help your people." She pauses again. "Instead of being like me." She sighs. "I don't know. I'm not so bad though. God might forgive me. I hope so."

The bus driver taps the breaks at her stop and the passengers shift forward and back as if to nod in agreement. The bus doors open, and she blows us a kiss. "Keep Winning!" she says and hops off.

I watch Aunty Lottie from the bus window as she walks down the sunlit sidewalk with her long black hair, wearing all white and glowing like an angel. The dream changes again, and I am out fishing with Will. He is picking the net when a killer whale swims to the boat. She speaks, "They'll steal anything."

There is an explosion and we look up to see boats chasing a pod of orcas through the pass, herding the young ones away from their pod. The dream changes and we see white men coming for Indian children. The children cry as they're put onto a truck and taken from their parents—away to boarding school.

The dream changes and we are staring at an orca from behind aquarium glass. When our eyes meet, we both see her endless days of aquarium life; the buckets of fish slopped to her at intervals.

"Have a Pop Tart," says a disembodied voice, and she opens her maw like a baby bird for 50 years.

We see her loneliness in that stunted world. And then we see what seems to be another whale, but somehow it isn't.

"It can't sing because it's not real," comes the voice again. "None of this is real; it's just a concrete fishbowl."

The orca swims away and when she swims back, she is Lottie, but somehow she isn't. She presses her palm to the glass, "Keep winning," she says and I wake.

Over Oregon the Flight Attendant Asks
If I'm Interested in Water
Jennifer Richter

> *I was wondering how you feel about your name being associated with a disaster.*
> —archived fan mail to Charles Francis Richter, creator of the magnitude scale

Over Oregon the flight attendant asks if I'm interested in water
and I nod at his tray of clear cups lined up like the carnival game

that won me a fish I named after myself oh like the Richter scale
people say in Oregon where tsunami trips kids up on spelling tests

some letters are absurd they ask the seismologist *which of these states*
should I move to but one begins *you're the only other Francis I know*

my teacher told me about you I hate my name they scream it at recess
I don't even have a middle name what do your friends call you and also

do earthquakes scare you like they do me yes thanks I'm very interested
in the unlikely event of water landing on our home thirty thousand

feet below when I chose to keep this name disaster hadn't occurred
to me but now our children drop cover hold on in school they raise

their hands to my husband's name on the first day the teacher isn't
sure who I belong to their hair matches exactly that class goldfish

with alarmed eyes if something happens how will strangers help me
find them my name will be useless my name will be news for years

that third grade fish has been living dying getting replaced overnight
though to the children it's always Charlie the seismologist's name

ended with him but his carbon-copied reply calls the boy son and
uses the word *wonder* when ours was lost in the children's museum

he'd looped back to the tsunami tank to methodically stack blocks
under a giant timer counting down to the wave that came so close

he couldn't hear me calling

The Ground at My Feet

Ann Stinson

I

I sit on a recently felled Douglas Fir and look around. It is early evening and the loggers, hard at work on the harvest since dawn, are gone for the day. Floaty gnats inhabit the slanting light.

A sword fern frond reaches out and touches my notebook. It merges with Oregon Grape, Salal, fir branches, cedar boughs and chunks of bark. The soil is dark and soft and airy. I touch it. I make three dark stripes on each of my cheeks. The soil is drier than I expect; my stripes are smudges.

I want to roll around in the newly exposed dirt and hear what it has to say. It smells rich and full of secrets. Everything has been opened up. Stories await my hearing. Does the soil know my brother's voice? Does the land remember his love? This forest was my growing ground from ten to eighteen, and now, years later, home again. How can I better hear what it has to say to me?

From my seat on the log, I observe a large old snag in the middle of the cut. We've left it as a perch for hawks and crows. The broken branches stand black against slow moving clouds backlit by the setting sun. In this gloaming, I listen to the trees.

At the edge of the cut lies Gemini Grove, six acres of majestic 100-year-old trees my sister-in-law Lou Jean and I have set aside. We go there for walks and contemplation, and the Grove shelters critters that like deep shade. It is also home to my brother Steve's tree, where we go to remember him.

As the harvest enters the third week, Lou Jean and I walk the wetland trail in the Grove. In the low spots, water stands at six inches. Last year's alder leaves line the bottom, and new lovage nudges through the surface. A long strand of green gray moss floats over my blue rubber boots. Later I look up the moss. Common name: Witches Hair Lichen; Latin: Alectoria sarmentosa. Lou Jean likes to gather and place it around the ceramic woodswoman holding some of Steve's ashes. She likes him to be warm.

We have hired a father and son team, Peter Sr. and Peter Jr. to do the logging. From the trail we can hear the grind and thump of their machines and then can see them beyond our 50- foot boundary. This logging has daylighted our trail, bringing sun into pockets of fern and old growth stumps sunken in deep shade for decades. Peter Sr.'s saw whines over the clearcut as we enter into a darker section of the Grove. A tree falls and shakes the ground.

Peter is hand-falling. These trees are too big for the modern-day cut-to-length processors most of the industry uses. I'm glad. This method is more personal, a more gracious relationship between faller and tree.

As Peter Sr. falls them, Peter Jr. walks down each tree with a chainsaw, cutting the branches close to the trunk. Next he climbs into a processor, a huge bright orange Doosan that cuts the tree into logs lengths. With another Doosan, a loader, he'll pick up the logs and place them on their truck.

The cedar is milled at Reichert Shake and Fencing, a family-owned mill just a mile and a half away. Other local mills process fir into two by fours, plywood, telephone poles.

Some of our Douglas Fir goes to Korea to be used in temples. These logs must be taller than 36 feet and larger than 32 inches top diameter. I wish all our trees went to such treasured purposes.

Douglas Fir logs with the fewest defects are exported to Japan for home-building while rougher logs we export to China where some are used to construct concrete forms. At least the imprint of the knotty wood grain stays embedded in the concrete, an echo of forest life from across the Pacific. I imagine traveling to Asia to see and touch the wood in its new home.

—<o>—

A sampling of defects used to grade export Douglas Fir.
> AS: Age Stain
> BT: Beaver Tail
> CF: Cat Face
> EK: Excessive Knots
> F: Fluted or Flared Butt
> FC: Freeze Crack
> HC: Heart Check
> OH: Off-Center Heart
> PR: Pitch Ring
> SB: Snow Break
> SK: Spike Knot
> SP: Spangle
> WS: Wind Shake

Another defect, known as "a school marm" is the fork in a treetop log. The current spec sheet for a Longview sawmill reads, "buck out school marms back to a single heart; no forked tops." As a former school teacher, I take offense at this even as I laugh.

We can sell the bucked-out school marms and other rough wood for pulp to make paper. We will keep leftover parts of the trees for firewood. Woodworking friends come to look at the burls, yew and other "hobby wood."

I discover that some wood from Pacific Northwest forests is used for coffins in rural China. The invitation to the monthly Lewis County Farm Forestry Association meeting announces an upcoming talk by the owner of Millwood, a company in Olympia that ships oversized trees for this purpose. I tell Dad we have to go. He gathers his 30-year-old Society of American Foresters clipboard and puts on his city clothes. I check to make sure the t-shirt he wears under his button down isn't frayed.

We drive to the Lewis County Courthouse and walk into the basement room where we have sat many times for talks about thinning, road building, planting alder, herbicide use, and surveying land boundaries. Dad is "the godfather" here; he and Steve both served as president of the association.

Rich Nelson from Millwood presents slides showing how wood gets from Tacoma to inland China. The wood he buys is big and rough and has many of the defects Weyerhaeuser will not take. Logs over 33 inches in diameter, spike knots, spangle, all these are acceptable for Millwood.

Provinces on the coast of China have outlawed burials; city dwellers must cremate their deceased. But in the countryside, families still want a coffin for a "soil funeral." Coffin design varies by region, but all require five thick boards about 24 inches wide. Many families prefer each board to be made from one tree; it helps the soul stay in the coffin.

I am pleased families want the otherwise rejected wood—material deemed unsuitable for plywood or two by fours—for the final resting place of their loved ones. The truth in myth trumps extreme rationality.

—◇—

One morning the rain ebbs and flows, slows and pounds on the metal roof above me; I lie listening. When it's just a whisper, I can hear the hum of Peter's saw, and the thump of his single-bit ax. I walk out to the logging site in the early afternoon with my notebook. On an old-growth stump sprouting huckleberry in its second life, I see Peter's coffee mug that reads, "sawdust is man glitter." The Canada Geese call, harsh and exciting. The Crowned Kinglets chirp. When I am writing, I notice more, I ask more questions. Peter asks, "Are you writing a book?" Father and son both want to show me things.

I take a video of Peter falling a tree on the bluff: an old open-grown fir tree called a hooter because its branches are good for birds. We are leaving the hooter next to it. He is almost finished, but he waves me over and instructs me to climb up in the loader and knock the tree down.

It is cold and pissing rain. I use Peter's knee and a pile of branches to get onto the loader's tracks, then up the metal ladder. Young Peter tells me which joysticks move the shovel in the right direction. A few swings knock the tree to the ground. With the grapple, I move it to a clear place for easy delimbing. I am nervous, excited, out of my element. Totally new, these movements are large, not subtle. Expansive. Room for breath and thought and limit testing.

We will plant this year's cut next spring. By March, fir, cedar, and pine seedlings will be growing at 9 feet intervals across twelve acres of land. We will start a new forest. Dad has been calculating the number of seedlings we'll need. 1970s calculator, a yellow legal pad, and a sharp pencil are his tools. We've decided to plant Western White Pine, Western Red Cedar and Douglas Fir. The cedar and pine are resistant to laminated root rot, present in the soil and exacerbated by climate change. Douglas Fir is not, but we will plant it in the ashes of burn piles in hopes that some will survive.

The trees grow, clean water flows, and deer, grouse, elk, and bear make the forest their home. The shade cools the salmon streams, and the growing branches act as carbon absorbers, soaking up light from the sun and carbon dioxide from the air to make sugars for their energy. No fertilizer, just one application of herbicide in 80 years of a stand's life. Dad's pickup has two bumper stickers: Wood is Good and Family Forests are a Salmon's Best Friend.

II

In the months that made up the year after my brother died, I memorized poems. I repeated them aloud as I put one foot in front of the other on forest trails. Words written down and folded to fit into my fleece pocket. Rain splattered, muddy, they live in the back of my notebook now—and in my breath and the back nooks of my mind—to be brought out when I need to ease restlessness. Mary Oliver and Emily Dickinson have become my internal friends.

> *"After a great pain a formal feeling comes." (ED)*
> *"I wanted to thank the mockingbird for the vigor of his song."(MO)*
> *"Tell the truth, but tell it slant." (ED)*
> *"The world offers itself to your imagination." (MO)*

Dickinson's work still resonates—I'm not sure whether it stays because of its darkness, or despite it, but *there's a certain slant of light that oppresses like the heft of cathedral tunes* . . . When my mind is racing, my pillow overly warm, I can summon the rhythms of these words and breathe them down to my toes. Arriving at the last stanza,

> *When it comes, the Landscape listens –*
> *Shadows – hold their breath –*
> *When it goes, 'tis like the Distance*
> *On the look of Death –*

I am in the shadows as they hold their breath, and see the slant of light come and go, leaving its distant mark. This mark is on Steve's face as I lie beside him and Lou Jean the night he's died. I touch his cheek, tentatively. I lay down next to her as she snuggles him. She's put his wedding ring on a chain around her neck. His grimacing, moaning and grasping —so hard to witness—has subsided to a look of softness, distant, but merciful.

Emily's crisp rhythms allow me access into the room of death, and they create a structured entry and a way back out. The repeated soft *"ths"* soothe me, and create a cocoon in which I can slumber. It's a fertile space, dark and warm and powerful.

—◦—

On the day that marks a year, I drive with Lou Jean and my husband Tom to each parcel of Cowlitz Ridge Tree Farm. We are in Lou Jean's black truck. From the rearview mirror hangs an eagle feather, a gift from a Hopi healer, one of the many healers on Steve's determined quest to rid his body of cancer. Next to my feet is a small shopping bag, "Taxco Sterling." Originally, it held "pretty shiny things" for Lou Jean from Steve's family forest advocacy trips to Washington DC. Now it holds some of Steve's ashes.

We drive east on Highway 12. Limby fir and sprawling big-leaf-maple line the road. Past the blueberry and tulip farms, up the hill to "Mossyrock," the largest of the timber parcels Steve loved. Lou Jean suggests we spread some ashes in the twelve-year-old alder stand planted in an old sloping field. The slope allows rain to slowly feed the alder roots. The sunlight passes through their oval leaves and patterns her tie-dyed t-shirt. Lou Jean reads a few lines of Wendell Berry, one of Steve's favorite authors:

> *And the world cannot be discovered by a journey of miles, no matter how long, but only by a spiritual journey, a journey of one inch, very arduous and humbling and joyful, by which we arrive at the ground at our own feet, and learn to be at home.*

Elk have roughened the bark of the slender alder stems with their rubbing. I uncurl my fingers and my handful of ash sifts down over the previous autumn's crumbling leaves. My palm, now empty, is still covered in a gray gritty dust. What do I do with it? To wipe it on my jeans seems crude, disrespectful. I just keep my hand open and still, not wanting to disturb the dust's pattern along my lifeline.

Down the grassy road back to the truck, we walk through firs that Steve planted thirty years ago. It's easy walking; lower branches have fallen away; the upper branches shade out underbrush. Only the sounds of ravens, hawks and squirrels break the silence. As I lock the red gate painted last September with Dad, I pick a trailing blackberry. It stains my fingertips still coated in Steve's ashes. I lick them and make a fingerprint at the top of the first page of my spiral notebook. I am taking notes. I need this day to stay with me forever. I must own this day and share with those who feel the hole of Steve's death.

We head back west on Highway 12, windows down, hot air blowing our hair. Up Jackson Highway to "Callison," the last place Steve supervised a harvest of fir, hemlock, and cedar. Tom reads Berry's words:

"arduous,"

"discover,"

"learn to be at home"

float in the air with thistle fluff. I take another handful of ashes to the cedar log where Dad, Lou Jean, and I, earlier this year, ate smoked oysters and saltines, resting from our work of slash burning, boundary marking, and tubing newly planted cedar. I sprinkle my ashes around the log so Steve can join us next time. Though I want them to stay visible, the ashes disappear into the dusty gravel and browned grass.

Callison is also the site of a yearly bounty of chanterelles hiding under waist high Salal. "Steve always found the most," says Lou Jean. We soon locate one of Steve's favorite mushroom picking spots. I read Berry's words:

"journey of one inch,"

"humbling,"

"joyful"

and they mix with the ashes. Here, the dust from my ashy palm stays visible on the green pointy leaves of Oregon Grape and Salal. After Lou Jean spreads her handful she shows me, in her open palm, a small screw. She says, "It's a part of Steve. From his broken ankle. I found the plate earlier."

Steve's death is a raw wound in wet ground after a 100-year old cedar falls in a windstorm: broken roots, exposed rocks, soil that has not seen the sun for decades. But a year has passed, and in the hole from the wind-thrown tree, there is new growth—stronger bonds between those gathering round. The new growth is not a consolation. It just is. And this growth is nothing like the tree, but without the destruction, it wouldn't be there. We will tend the tender shoots.

—◇—

Simple Berry Buckle: butter, eggs, sugar, lemon, flour and berries. Picking the berries is the best part—Steve died with blackberry scratches on his hands.

And the vines still grow, trailing blackberries low to the ground. New vines stretch along the edge of a clearcut now filling with four-year-old pine, fir and cedar, and foxglove, mullein, and daisies. It was Steve's favorite spot and is still full of fruit; next year the shade from the growing trees might not let in enough sunlight. The berries' dark purple juices stain my fingers.

My favorite trove this summer is a broken-down cedar log, decaying for 50-60 years, its red flesh webbed with vines, each bearing five or six plump berries. A Pileated woodpecker drums nearby, a hummingbird whirs in the fireweed. I'm so determined to pick a berry hiding under a salal leaf, I get nettles on my chin. Steve feels so near I can almost hear him chuckling.

An hour of picking and my container is full. I walk back home in my hickory shirt and Carhartts, my arms and legs unpierced by the thorns. The berry juices paint the batter red. The oven that baked Steve's last pie plumps and goldens the cake. Our fractured but mending family digs through cream to the warm buckle and finds Steve's berries from the young forest.

Neighborhood Profiles

Rhienna Renée Guedry

One is the man I've seen hurling a
tennis ball against the walls of his own home
        he once threw himself down on
our sidewalk to attract a crowd
while his bag of grocery store red apples
                                    emptied and rolled

One is the woman who chatters by force
her mouth splayed open,   wide
for the dentist, an ear-pop on a plane
an exclamation point
she details her cardigan's origin story, mends it
points to lime green vintage thread

One is shaped like an egg he walks
with his hands deep in brown pockets
strides   like a   metronome
keeps busy retrieving the

one item he forgot from the store, back
on the bus, pays the fare again like a new day

When two of our black cats turned up dead
the same day   we suspected one, told none

Oakdale

Tim Greenup

There were rumors that someone had buried a baby in the woods around Mud Lake. That you wouldn't have to dig far to find it. We took to the trees and kicked up dead leaves hoping to be the first to uncover the body. There was me, Mikey, Jason, my sister Sarah, and the other, older Sarah we all called Big Sarah. The kids of Granada Avenue in Oakdale Minnesota. Who knows what they imagined the dead baby to look like, we never went as far as to describe it to one another, but I imagined a sunken, shriveled thing, skin the color of a dried pig's ear, with no eyes wearing a yellow bonnet and frilled sundress, like the parents had gotten the baby dressed for Easter Mass and decided instead to bury it alive.

The woods were not a sprawling expanse of timber but a cluster of trees that hugged the edge of the lake, large enough for a child to get lost in but small enough to know. An adult could make a lap around the lake in an hour, but adults never went into the woods. They were busy clipping coupons for Folgers Coffee and chicken pot pies, ceremoniously folding them, gently placing them in an empty pickle jar on the kitchen counter. Adults never asked us about the woods. They knew we spent most of our time there, but the understanding seemed to be that whatever happened in the woods was a private kid thing. We appreciated this courtesy. No one needs to know precisely what someone else does with their time. If we wanted to disclose that Jason spotted a garter snake, or Mikey sliced up a worm with his Swiss Army Knife, we could, but we never did.

The woods were a graveyard of forgotten things: Snails, crawdad exoskeletons, old cutlery that escaped someone's Fourth of July barbecue and mysteriously wound up in the mud by the shore. As far as we were concerned, anything we found there belonged to us. We placed our findings in pencil boxes in our bedroom. Those boxes were full of stray buttons, unused erasers, birthday cards, pencils with our names on them, rocks shaped like organs. Things for which we had no earthly use, yet we kept them as tokens of our having been alive.

One afternoon I found a dead turtle in the woods. Not realizing it was dead, I took it home and placed it in a white bucket of hose water. I set the bucket on top a cinder block retaining wall and sat down next to it. We waited in the sun together, the turtle and I. My dad mowed the lawn. I felt the retaining wall scrape the back of my hairless legs. Dad wore a red trucker cap embroidered with the word Cozumel. He and my mom had gone scuba diving there one Christmas while my sister and I stayed at our great uncle's house eating frozen pizzas and doing the same *ALF* puzzle over and over again. My father had a thick mustache and dark sunglasses. His stomach hung over the waistband of his maroon Minnesota Gopher shorts. He was a welder and accustomed to the heat, his body leaking liquids without his realizing it. He had the shape of a man who every day after work drank a couple bottles of Michelob Genuine Draft and ate half a bag of corn chips, which he did.

I loved that Dad's lawnmower was a Snapper and bore a picture of a turtle on it. He mowed the lawn with more focus than he ever showed toward anything, making multiple diagonal sweeps of the front and side yard, so that when he was done the grass angled in such a way that our yard became a green wave. It was clear he had a distinct, guiding philosophy about the right way to mow the lawn but he never told anyone about it. This too was a private thing.

He cut the engine. "What's in the bucket?"

"Baby turtle," I said.

He wiped the sweat from his head with a thick, hairy forearm. "Got a name?"

"Jeremy."

He nodded in approval and kicked the engine back on. I felt validated. Jeremy sank to the bottom of the bucket. I waited in the sun for anything to happen. Dad cut the grass. When I got hot and bored, I decided to play guns. I gathered pistols and uzis with orange tips into a black duffle bag and crawled into the back of our pickup truck and closed the topper. I listened to the muffled hum of the lawnmower and rested my head on the metal wheel well.

Every car that drove past I filled with bullet holes. The cars would swerve across our neighbor's lawn—the neighbor my father disliked for playing music too loud—and smash through the garage door. Some exploded there, setting the house aflame. Others would plow all the way through the garage and into the backyard, barreling up and down small hills toward the creek, where the car would eventually slam into a tree trunk and leak gas and oil into the water until it, too, would explode.

Satisfied, I went inside for a Pepsi and drank it over ice at the kitchen table. My father was there too, slathering saltines with cream cheese.

I checked on Jeremy again.

"Anything happening?" my father said, dumping grass clippings into a large, hazy pile beside the garage.

"Nope."

Jeremy was still at the bottom of the bucket hiding in his shell.

My father would get frustrated with us kids in the summertime for coming and going from the house too much, tracking mud on the carpet and letting out all the air conditioning. Without any notice or discussion he started locking us out of the house. I pounded on the back door and screamed into the door jamb as if Jason Voorhees had risen slowly from the lake, tromped through the woods and our backyard in deliberate approach—so certain was my slaughter I couldn't help but imagine the creative methods he might use to mangle my small body. The door stayed closed.

We had no idea where in the woods to look for the baby's body, so we looked everywhere. We were young—five, six, seven. We had no strategy. We wanted the dead baby to find us as much as we wanted to find the dead baby. But we stuck to the woods and watched the ground for signs. I even found signs in my bedroom. On my dark oak dresser, my mom one day propped up a couple porcelain dolls with long black eyelashes. One wore a sailor cap and navy blue shorts. A thin, pink grin painted on its face suggested detached bemusement. The other doll wore a similar expression but was fashioned after a French clown, white face paint and white pantaloons. I'm not sure why she installed these dolls in my room or where they came from or whether they held any history or meaning for her. I never asked her about them. It wasn't my place to question my mother's choices. Most nights I woke to them staring down at me, their faces lit by the orange glow of my night light. It was too much. I would yank them from the dresser and throw them beside the bathroom trash can.

Each afternoon, my mother returned them to their post without saying a word to me about it.

One January night we came home late from swim lessons at the YMCA and found our house had been robbed. We opened the door and heard something drop. We went into the kitchen and found my mother's jewelry box scattered across the yellow linoleum. The paper blinds to our sliding back door were shaking. The wind came in through the opening and chilled the air. We clung to each other and looked into the backyard for an explanation. At first, we couldn't make out anything—the world was pitch black. Someone flipped a switch and flooded it with light. The sudden flash blinded us for a time, and then it revealed heavy boot prints in the snow. They faded into the tall trees of the woods.

That same winter the mother of the kidnapped boy, Jacob Wetterling, came and cried for us in the gymnasium of my elementary school. It had been months since her son disappeared during his bikeride home from the video store. (He had rented *Naked Gun*). The entire student body sat cross-legged on the gym floor in awe of her grief. She didn't want us to be taken from our lives the way Jacob had been taken from his. She didn't want our mothers and fathers to spend sleepless nights driving through small Minnesota towns looking for a bike, a red sweatshirt, a mud-covered shoe. She didn't want us to float through a black unknown for eternity shouting our parents' names. She wanted us to know that we were young and that at any moment we could be ripped from everything we knew. The man doing it would be a teacher, a dentist, a factory worker.

We believed her, but we also believed someday Jacob would return to his life. He'd be found in the basement of an old house on the other side of the state, shaken up and skinnier but still more or less the same Jacob. All of Minnesota clung to that hope for 27 years.

The woods promised so much but never gave us exactly what we wanted. Our interest in the dead baby faded when one of us heard from someone who'd heard from someone else's dad, there was a snapping turtle on the south end of the lake with a shell the size of a manhole cover. Bolstered by recent news stories about mutated frogs being discovered near the 3M plant in Cottage Grove, we willed the massive snapper into existence. We wanted to catch it and train it to protect us from a world we barely understood.

I imagined standing on its spiky shell and riding the beast like a Variflex skateboard across the asphalt streets of Oakdale. It would shred the half-dozen psycho sexual perverts that populated the three-block walk to school and who were waiting for their moment to snatch me by my backpack and pull me into a burgundy sedan and drive me to a nearby field, frantically trample down the tall stalks of corn or wheat and make me undress at gunpoint. No longer. When the turtle finished with the man with the cleft palate or the 50 year old bachelor who works third shift and wears plastic double-bar glasses with blue smoked lenses, he will look like pulled pork in a rich K.C. barbecue sauce.

I regularly stood on the shore waving my butterfly net through the water in hopes of snagging the turtle and pulling it to land and enlisting its divine powers of protection, my own gentilic gollum. The net returned one day with a large tear in it. I reasoned the turtle had snapped swiftly through the cheap netting and swam deeper down into the lake, indifferent to my fear. I was alone on the edge of the woods. The tall tops of the birch trees soon extinguished any remaining sunlight. I hurried to gather my things from the wet ground at my feet. Sudden and decisive, night descended.

Goslings

Sam Robison

they drowned in the mud
like they might've in
nature, someone says
as in tarpit, as in sinkhole

fell into the shallow hole
couldn't climb out for the rain
drowned in the mud there
and in their fear there
cold, wet

found them in the morning
one morning, kingdom of daylight
draining through trees
their bodies rolled through mud
little-caramel-apple-like, little beaks
dimly open, drinking up soot

a dead thing is not a novel thing here
violence stitches this beauty together

every bed dug a kind of violence
every row planted a new unnatural laceration
an imposition of bad order, another
wound to dress

still, often death is happened upon
and its drama is recapitulated in an instant
                their fall there
                their trying to clamber out
                their failure, their slips and
                mother goose yells, father
                goose hisses, a scene
                of bird-brained helplessness, a
                fever of helplessness snuffed out
                by boredom, a slow, gurgling death

two gosling bodies, wrapped in mud, dried now
caking a little, there, unexpected and
the grief absorbs the air all around you
for one flickering frame

and then gloves, then shovel

Nubes

Alexander Ortega

De Pedrito, desde las Nubes

Felipe,

After you and David rocket-boosted me from the trampoline, I flew up and up into las nubes. I landed on one—it looked like vanilla ice cream that late afternoon, and it felt like a chilly pillow. In the distance there was a tunnel, all made of nubes. I crawled to the edge of la nube and peeked over to see our itty-bitty vecindario and the waterpark, then the big buildings farther away, all a long ways to the ground. I walked through the tunnel.

I was scared when the two of you forced me up to the sky. Like Mamá says, todavía estoy pequeño. And now I was scared walking through that tunnel, even though it was pink—tan bonito como la paletería—but it didn't taste like cotton candy, only like nieve. I reached a big room, walls and a ceiling of nubes, which seemed empty at first. I sensed someone behind me.

I turned and saw a tall lady with a chalk-white face. I screamed, stumbling to the ground. I cried in fear, scooting on my behind—even her lips were white. She never moved her mouth, like when the principal speaks on the intercom, but she told me not to be afraid. She was bald, with a white gown draped over her body down past her feet, touching the floor of las nubes. At least I think she had a body underneath. She looked like she was gliding as she came close to me. I cried more. Quiero mi mamá! I said with tears wetting my cheeks. She said she knew that Mamá loves me. But she said I was sad at home, too.

I let the tall woman hold me. There were arms or something underneath her gown. She let me tell her about all the times you've made me cry then called me chillón. When I put stickers on your guitar, I just wanted to make it look even cooler—I wanted you to tell me, Está bien padre. But you threw my cars in the garbage! It still makes me sad. Why are you always so mean, Felipe? I just want to be cool like you. Why do you always punch me to give me a dead arm and tell me I'm adopted? Why do you tell me I'm gay? I just want to play with you and David. It hurts my feelings when you slap me.

The white lady led me behind a puff of cloud. There was a flying saucer in an even bigger room of nubes behind that secret puff. I wished you could see it. There were flashing buttons and levers for huge screens, like on Power Rangers. The white lady took me to the middle where a tall man—all white like her but with a curly, black beard—stood in a beam of blue light. I slept in a bunk bed in that room.

The next day, he woke me up and asked if I wanted to see my life—he talks without mov-ing his mouth, too. I said I didn't know, but he turned on a screen anyway. He showed the bad stuff, the mean things you've done to me. He showed good stuff, too, like when you walked me home from school and gave me a Mewtwo Pokémon card. I forgot you did that—the card's still in my pocket.

But then, Felipe, he showed me when you and David rocket-boosted me. You two just laughed and high-fived. You weren't even worried if I'd come back.

So I'm not.

Eres mi hermano, pero me odias.

The man with the beard said I could go with them. He and the white lady told me they fly through space to other planets. They find beings from the universe who they see have greatness. They told me I'm one of the great ones and that I have a pure heart. They'll take me to their home planet and guide me to become a leader to fix other planets in the universe.

They're going to give me a shot so I can sleep for the long trip. I hate shots, and I don't get why I can't just stay awake with them. They say it lasts light years. I wish I could show you all the lit-up buttons where the white lady flies the saucer—they're organized by color, like an electronic rainbow. It reminds me of when we'd jump on the tramp until the streetlights came on, especially when the sun's going down but you can feel how bright all the lights are, and the taillights on the neighbors' cars look like robot eyes.

They're giving me the shot soon, Felipe. Dile a mi mamá que también la voy a extrañar.

— Pedrito

—◇—

Megayega!

History.

Megayega was actually named Magdalena. Her husband called her by her name, and her toddler imitated him, calling her Megayega instead of Mamá or Mommy. When Megayega's husband went to war, servicemen arrived knocking three times at her door. Upon receiving their news of her husband's death, Megayega plummeted into melancholia. She neglected her baby and drank excessively. Eventually, her baby began to starve and would cry desperately: "Megayega! Megayega!"

The toddler tapped, hit, and slammed objects around the apartment, trying to get Megayega's attention. He shook his heart-shaped rattle angrily. In a drunken stupor, Megayega shoved red grapes down her baby's throat then smothered him with a pillow once she could no more take his wails. She swallowed a bottle of pills with a fifth of whiskey and died in her bed. Strangely, her landlord found her body with a pacifier in her mouth. After the police searched the apartment, they found thousands of dollars stowed away inside one of her pillows.

Why summon.

Summoning Megayega is a game. When you've successfully summoned her, you'll feel claustrophobic as she comes close, and your face will feel hot. To abate her, you can either take a shot of whiskey or swallow a grape whole. If you don't, the heat and claustrophobia will become nigh unbearable. However, if you withstand the side effects of drunkenness, the discomfort of potentially choking, or Megayega's abuse, you'll find money hidden under furniture, in parking lots, or left for you when you awake in the morning, etc.

Juan Caramelo.

Juan Caramelo was hard on cash. He was an inveterate drinker, so he summoned Megayega. He downed a shot with panache at the first sensation of heat, then took swigs of whiskey for the rest of the first day to keep Megayega at bay. He kept it going for months, and the amounts of money he found exponentiated. He eventually moved to Vegas with enough money to invest at the tables. He won big.

Warning.

Never try to summon a ghost or demon. If you perform a summoning ritual incorrectly, the spirit could haunt you forever, which could lead to possession and even death. Performance of any steps of a summoning are also highly dangerous. You could pass out and injure yourself from the intense sensations of overheating and claustrophobia—especially if a summoning is not undertaken correctly. Or possibly worse, if a spirit, demon, or ghost isn't banished properly, you may have to live with it past the timeframe you initially intended. Don't try to summon Megayega.

Gloria Melendez.

Gloria Melendez, a single mother like Megayega, loved her baby. She was fired from her job and decided to summon Megayega for some easy money. She vomited after her second shot of the summoning, and heard her baby wailing in her crib. When she arrived, a serpentine shadow hovered over her babe, licking it with a forked tongue. She commanded it to leave, but soon discovered that her baby had died of shock.

Materials.

To summon/banish Megayega, you'll need the following:

- ❑ Whiskey plus a shot glass
- ❑ Pillow with a pillowcase on it
- ❑ Bottle of pills
- ❑ Pacifier
- ❑ Red grapes

Preparation.

Ensure the following prior to summoning Megayega:

- ❑ You must be alone.
- ❑ Since it will be dark, determine where you'll sit in your kitchen in advance.
- ❑ You must turn off all sources of light in your home. There must be very little to no light, especially no daylight.

Note on name.

Take note that stating the name of Megayega before proceeding with the process could alter the summoning. Such an alteration may cause Megayega or some other demon to possess you instead of playing a game. In fact, never speak the name of a demon aloud, for even the utterance of a name could attach them to you, your possessions, or your loved ones near you.

Instructions.

Follow these directions to summon Megayega:

- ❏ Knock three times at your front door, from the inside.
- ❏ Walk to your seat in your kitchen area.
- ❏ Pour a shot of whiskey into a shot glass and shoot it in one gulp.
- ❏ Shake a bottle of pills.
- ❏ Swallow a grape whole.
- ❏ Wash it down with another shot.
- ❏ Move to a bedroom.
- ❏ Put your head inside a pillowcase with a pillow inside it.
- ❏ Lie on your back, press the pillow into your face, and yell "Megayega!" three times.
- ❏ Go to sleep with a pacifier in your mouth.

When you awake, you'll know that the summoning worked if you hear a rattle or shaking pill-bottle noises. This is Megayega's baby calling for Megayega's attention. You'll know she's closer when you hear nondescript taps, clunks, or erratic white noise in general. She's quite close when you hear a wet, mouthy sucking noise. That's Megayega calming herself with a pacifier.

Be sure to have whiskey and grapes on your person at all times. Soon enough, your face may feel hot, and you'll feel the space around you constrict. If

Megayega wins a match, you'll likely pass out. Sometimes, Megayega may steal money from you as well. That doesn't mean the game is over, however; she's just won that match, and you'll need to banish her.

Duane Salazar.

Duane Salazar couldn't catch a break. His wife had left him and took his savings, and Megayega was too quick for him. He kept passing out, and he'd concussed himself after too many collisions with furniture or other nearby, happenstance objects. He began attempts to banish Megayega, but Megayega would assail him. Neighbors saw Duane in his front yard, splashing whiskey on his face and sucking on a pacifier, and they called the authorities. When he passed out in the middle of the street, he was arrested. Puzzled doctors soon institutionalized him, issuing diagnoses of schizophrenia and narcolepsy. Nurses consistently found dollar bills in his straightjacket.

Banishing.

To banish Megayega, swallow three grapes in succession and take three shots of whiskey. Then rattle a pill bottle aggressively. Suck on a pacifier.

—<o>—

A Real Man

The Coco Man threw me into his sack just like my parents said he would—all for being mean to my sister and not praying. That frigid Noche Buena, the rough burlap chafed against my skin, and I kicked and punched. He lashed me with his whip. I wore myself out and fell asleep.

I awoke when he dropped me, and I scurried out of the bag. He was draped in a brown, ragged, hooded cloak. He pointed to the snowcapped mountains at the edge of the basin and told me, "Go." I began to cry and he repeated his command, shaking his finger. When I didn't go, he fell to his knees and brought his bruised, scabbed hands to his face and also wept.

Bemused, I asked him why he was crying.

"The Devil. He's mean. I can't hurt children anymore, even bad ones like you."

Through his sobs, he related how he barely remembered his parents, only that they'd held him tight before the Devil stole him. The Devil raised him in a cage and fed him gruel until he could carry a five-year-old. He'd scourge the Coco Man, despite his finding plenty of bad children to toss from cliffs. The Coco Man was broken. I pitied him.

"Your bed looked warm," he said. "I've never had a bed."

"Coco Man," I said, "I can't do anything about your parents, but I can show you how to be a real man if you take me home." I wasn't a man, I was ten, but I knew what a real man was. "First give me a coat and shoes because it's freezing, burro."

He sliced up his sack, draped it over me, and fished some shoes out of his cloak.

He made us an adobe hut. My parents wouldn't let the Coco Man live with us, even in the toolshed. We decided I'd teach him how to be a real man, then he'd let me go home. Hopefully my parents wouldn't miss me for a while and wouldn't beat me.

"To be a real man," I said, "the first thing to learn is how to ride a four-wheeler."

The Jaramillo family had three, so I hot-wired one at night, and we rode back into la sierra. The Coco Man puttered around on it, slow—"I think a horse would be better," he said—and didn't understand that it had power steering. He drove in circles. I wanted to get out of the snow, so I told him he was doing great. The only thing he probably had ever been good at was abducting and tossing kids, poor bastard.

I was going to teach him how to build a fire, but he could do that by snapping his fingers. I threw a rock at him. "I've been freezing this whole damn time, burro!"

Next was teaching him how to shave. He melted a frozen spring for its reflection, and I used his dull knife on my budding moustache. I pushed back his hood, which felt crusty and weighed heavily on his head. His face was twisted in knots, bruises, and blemishes. Disgusted, I guided him through scraping whiskers off of the right side of his jaw. He did the other half by himself while I threw rocks at birds.

At the hut, he didn't make me pull his boots off. I told him he needed to slap my head and make me scrub the floor like a dad. He said he couldn't.

"Coco Man, you're not gonna kill me—you just gotta show me who's boss."

We heard a rap at the door. The Devil entered. He looked like any old cowboy except he had pink, swollen horns on his forehead.

"You won't have any luck with him, 'jito," he said, putting his hand on my shoulder. As the Devil spoke, the Coco Man backed into the corner of our hut. "All he's good for is hauling children and tossing them off cliffs."

"He's my burro now, cabrón." I spat.

The Coco Man whimpered.

"His mamá was a whore, a bruja. He's a walking curse—you'd have better luck with a goat," the Devil said, motioning outside as a goat bleated.

I kicked the Devil right in his crotch. He winced a little—I saw it in his eyes—then he smiled, said fine by him, and left us.

"No llores," I said angrily to the Coco Man. "The next thing you've gotta do to be a man is get drunk at a bar and beat someone. My dad's a real man—he's the best at it."

I knew that I wouldn't be able to waltz into the bar by the highway, so I had the Coco Man carry me inside in another sack. I whispered that I'd tell him what to say as he sat down, sitting me on his lap inside the sack.

"Give me whiskey," he said to the bartender.

A shot glass slid across the bar top.

The Coca Man said, "I'll start a tab."

I kicked his ribs and he grunted. He shot the whiskey and hacked. "Gimme another shot," he hissed through his labored breathing. He drank a second and a third.

I told the Coco Man that we didn't have money, so he'd have to beat the bartender with his whip. The whip cut through the air with a swoosh, and the bartender wailed as the Coco Man lashed him.

I climbed out of the sack and clung to the Coco Man's neck, peering over his shoulder at the unconscious bartender. Cowboy boots clacked through the bar door behind us.

The Coco Man collapsed to the floor, caterwauling.

The Devil said, "I won't trifle with you anymore, Coco Man, pathetic burro."

He turned to me. "Cabroncito, it's a cold world out there, but you've got the fire to be a real man."

I understood and embraced him like a father. He sat me on his shoulders and strode to the nighttime sierra as I gripped his horns.

Don't be the Bear

Shannon Amidon

Yesterday a bear and our four-year-old
had a standoff at the kitchen slider. Neither

won exactly: both ran away. We blamed barbecue
from the night before, and the bright sunshine

after the long, dark winter. We just forgot,
the way the bear forgot there were people.

But today I'm at the lake, and there are three fishermen,
one brown bat clinging low to a sugar maple, and a fistful

of mysterious sequins on the ground, confetti mimicking
water beneath a moody sky: first nothing, then light.

And my oldest, 9, is reading on a screen, but it's reading
so I'm okay with that for now, happy, because maybe

I'm doing a pretty good job, because maybe now that
it's spring, and the daffodils have opened along the worn edges

of our old house, the house where my father grew into
my father, and the ice dams are not giving us so much trouble,

and the air pushing its way into our waiting lungs is damp
with future, maybe now I can find my husband beneath

his piles of newspapers and final exams, and take him to me
like the old days in our upstairs bedroom in Spokane,

a canopy of Norway maples above, a craft beer on the bedside
table, some music. Like the days when more of us were living,

when more of us longed for recognition, or money, or babies,
and more of us had less fear of time, before all the cancer,

or the suicide, when we shopped for things according to
their longevity first, and their beauty second. Waste: ever

forgetting grace, ever chasing whatever it is that the young

chase before their young come down the first slippery
river of humanity. So I remind myself: Don't be the bear.

Don't forget that the beautiful people make the beautiful smells,
that most doors open in every season, and nobody wins forever.

A Beginner's Guide to That Perfect Beach Body

Joaquin Fernandez

It will already be dark by the time you get to the beach house. The spare key will still be safe under the planter, guarded by the innumerable green, spiky tongues of the aloe your mother swears by. The air conditioner will start up with a sigh, sluggish after months of disuse. The refrigerator will be empty except for a single mummified carrot that you will never throw out and two half bottles of your mother's chardonnay that you will let yourself drink almost immediately. When you check your phone, you'll find a message from her wondering casually, but for the third time that day, how long you think you'll be planning on staying. Nothing in the house will want you there, least of all yourself.

It's important to sleep in your clothes that first night. It's important to not eat after the six-hour drive from Atlanta to Clearwater. It's important to drink the two half bottles of chardonnay while the air conditioner murmurs at you disapprovingly as you scroll through your ex-husband's Instagram with shaky fingers, terrified to hit the like button. Because you don't like anything right now. Not even your mother's emergency cigarettes, stale and stolen from the laundry room closet and chain-smoked while you white-knuckle your phone to keep yourself from stomping out to the surf in your bare feet and bathrobe, and sending the thing skipping into the Gulf just to watch it sink. You tell yourself things will be better in the morning. Except that's the same thing you've been telling yourself every night for the past three months.

In the morning, things aren't any better. In the morning, things aren't anything, because you sleep until twelve-thirty, and when you come to, you find yourself squinting against the scream of a headache. In the all-day sulk that follows, you order pizza and watch nature shows in your bathrobe while the ocean ebbs and flows sixty feet behind you. You check your bank account. You email your ex-husband's lawyer. You finally text back your mother. You tell her that you're fine because she needs you to be fine. Every year she and your father renew their membership to the aquarium in St. Petersburg and every year they get a calendar full of dolphins and otters and manatees. You take the calendar off the kitchen wall and spread it open on the coffee table in front of the TV where Martin Sheen's pretending to be the president. Your mother has texted you a date. You flip the calendar back two pages and mark it. You look at the calendar and you count down the days until your thirty-ninth birthday. You look at the calendar and add up the days you spent married. You divide it into months. You organize it by year. You simplify the fraction of the life you've spent. You can't bring yourself to say wasted. You can't bring yourself to say lost. The sun goes down while you're in a dark room looking into a graphing calculator.

On the first day that you run, you don't run. At five a.m. you shuffle to the beach in the misty Florida night and find that you're not alone. It's summer in Clearwater and you can feel that warm petri dish breeze coming off the ocean, something briny and alive, gestating in the dark, evolving for longer than Florida's been Florida. Growing up here, they teach you that Florida has sunk underwater four or five times while glaciers melted and refroze and the oceans rose and fell and rose again. When you were little, you would stand where you're standing now and imagine the endless ocean flooding up to meet you, pooling above your little sandals, rising past your knees, water rushing over the shoulder straps of your one-piece while you held your breath. When you were little, you thought it would be thrilling. You thought everyone would be laughing while it happened.

On the first day that you run, you don't run. Rather, you're going to stand on the beach in shorts and sneakers, just past the reach of the tide, under a moonless sky while a traffic of shadows passes before you. They're going to wave and nod, friendly in a way that's surprising. They're going to whisper *Hi!* into the foggy pre-dawn ether when they see you. You're never going to learn any of their names, but as long as you're there, you're going to be one of them. They dot the beach in groups and pairs, jogging, running, limping into view, then past, away and further, silhouettes in the dark like an exercise in perspective.

After a few minutes of standing there, you're going to walk. You're going to put your headphones in, but not play anything. You're just going to listen to the waves. You're going to get lost in the dark while the ocean pulls and crashes, pulls and crashes, pulls and crashes against the beach, sighing, content, and waiting for you to walk in. When your eyes adjust to the dark, you'll notice the crabs. They're going to scatter as you pass, specks and shadows underfoot, hurrying home in a ceaseless diagonal. You stand and watch them for a moment, scurrying back to their burrows after a long night of criss-crossing and you let yourself feel a little jealous.

The next day you're going to walk and the day after that you're going to walk a little faster and faster and faster and by the end of a week, someone might even call it a jog. Everyday, you're going to limp back home a little later and a little less breathless. Everyday, you're going to eat bowl after bowl of cereal in front of the TV, cozy and sore in your bathrobe. You're going to text your friend Janine, who's really more of a friend of a friend, but her husband left last year, so you're practically related. She reached out before you left. That is, she reached out before you put your things in storage and got in the car and didn't know where else to go. When you text her, it feels like you're in the same book, but she's a few chapters ahead. When you text her, it feels like you're allowed to scream when everyone else needs you to whisper. After two weeks at your parent's beach house, she texts you.

She sends: *It's time.*

You send: *For what?*

She sends: *For whatever comes next.*

You put down the phone and check your bank account. You tap the keys of your graphing calculator. You tap them again. You go to the calendar and flip the pages back from manatee to dolphin to otter. It's important that you let yourself pour a drink at this point, something dark and toxic, far stronger than your mother's chardonnay. You double check the calendar. You double check your math. You need whatever comes next to come soon. You open your laptop and start through want ads for anything you can do from home. It's important that you don't have to leave the house. It's important that you don't have to see people. It's important to pour yourself a second drink. It's important to pour a third.

When the package arrives, you open it with a rush of panic. You feel seen in a way that reminds you you've been hiding. Inside the package is another package, a case of something mummified in bubble wrap and scotch tape. You open it, careful to pop as many plastic bubbles as you can, and find six glass jars along with a note.

Hope this helps, –Janine.

The jars are covered in a language you don't recognize, bright colors punctuated by happy, cartoon fish. You text Janine and hold the jar up to the light, examining it like a code to be deciphered.

She texts: *It's for your skin! I've been using it for a month and I'm practically glowing!*

And: *My niece gets it for practically nothing!*

Then: A picture of her smiling face. Janine is a little older, on the other side of forty-five, and she looks incredible. Her skin is brighter. The crows feet and laugh lines she wears with pride in photos have receded, giving her face an airbrushed quality that makes you think of magazine covers in the 90's. You let your bathrobe slide off and inspect yourself in front of the mirror. You do not look airbrushed. You let yourself open the jar and inspect its contents. The cream is a pale pink, smooth and speckled with a pleasant smell like ocean water and eucalyptus. You look back at yourself in the mirror. You would not be on a magazine cover in the 90's. On the couch in your underwear, you put on a documentary about octopuses while you cover yourself in pale, pink cream. On the TV, an octopus is trapped in a jar underwater. Ocean water and eucalyptus are seeping into your pores. It's on your thighs. It's on your face. It's in the air you breathe. On the TV, the octopus is unscrewing the jar underwater and making its way out.

A week later you're doing data entry. You build Excel spreadsheets while nature shows drone on behind you. You can feel your mind going numb while you stare past your laptop, out the window to the beach, past the surf and into the slow July boil of the Gulf. You can feel your eyes shimmer with the mirage heat of the Florida summer while you bundle your bathrobe tight against the chill of the air conditioner.

By your third week of running, you actually start running. You move through the night, panting in the dark like a whispered secret. You begin to keep pace. You begin to recognize other runners on sight. When the sun comes up, you let yourself sit. You let yourself bury your toes in the sand while the ocean laps your feet clean. You let your sweat evaporate while you watch the other runners walk off the beach and back towards their real life. You watch old women in threes and fours carpooling back to their retired lives in jackets and visors. You study the curve and bounce of the sorority girls in bikinis, willing yourself not to be jealous. Even in college, that was never your body. Even when you met your ex-husband, your middle was soft and when you close your eyes, you can still feel him wrapping his arms around you from behind. You can still feel his fingernails grazing down the planted trunks of your legs. He's never going to touch you again, but there, alone on the beach, just for a moment, you let yourself miss his fingernails.

Janine texts: *You never get over it, but you get used to not getting over it.*

She says: *Tinder works, as long as you're honest. That includes with yourself.*

And: *Running helps. So does meeting new people. You can't just live in your bathrobe.*

It's almost eight am and you're back from a run, stretching and flexing under the too-hot steam of a shower on the last day of July. You've been running almost every day for a month. Real running with slick hair and burning thighs and the kind of deep lung grunting breaths that send crabs and college girls scattering while you plow through. The kind of running that leaves you gasping and ugly and stronger than you could have ever imagined. In the mirror after your shower, with your bathrobe open, you smooth the pink cream onto every inch of you, your fingers gliding over every curve and crease. The bags under your eyes have disappeared, though you hardly sleep, regularly waking before five without an alarm. The skin at your neck is smooth where it had begun to sag. The worry lines under your widow's peak are gone as is the cellulite that used to live behind your thighs. You admire them in the mirror over your shoulder while you rub them down with pink cream, smooth and strong and taut with muscle. You stare at yourself for a long time, longer than you have in years. You watch a smile bloom on your face when you realize that you have started to become unrecognizable.

You text Janine: *I'm really starting to see a change!*

And: *I think I'm ready for whatever comes next!*

She responds: *I hope we both are.*

In the mornings, you stretch while coffee brews, but you're always still sore. You've started to love it, the spice of pain simmering in the background of your life. It feels like strength. It feels like growth. At noon you take a break from spreadsheets to crack your back after hours of sitting. Upside-down and backwards on a yoga ball, you relish the broken glass crackle of your body working itself out. In the evenings, you watch nature shows and fail to reach the two stubborn knots at your back. The more your body hurts, the more you get used to it being hurt. On the last day of July, you think about what Janice said. *You get used to not getting over it.* Alone after weeks of being alone, you think about what Janice said. *Tinder works.*

The pictures you take for your profile are surprising. You didn't expect to look that good. You didn't expect your smile to feel so genuine. You let yourself admire them for a minute before adding the caption *Recently single, badly in need of a massage.* You send them to Janine.

She responds: *Whatever you're doing, don't stop!*

You spend an hour swiping right with a glass of wine in your hand before falling into an uneasy sleep. When you wake up, your back is worse. You stretch, in bed, in the dark, in agony. You listen for the crash of waves past the hum of the air conditioner. You sit at the foot of your bed and think about your sneakers in the closet in front of you. You think about the stacked pillows behind you and the ache at your back. Whatever you're doing, don't stop. You don't let it keep you off the beach. When you look at your phone in the dark, you see that Janine has texted you.

She says, *Has it started? Don't worry, it's easier after the first month.*

And, *I took up swimming and I've never felt better.*

Then, *I know it hurts. And I'm sorry.*

A few nights later, you meet a man for drinks. He's younger. Younger than you, much younger than your ex-husband and when he shows up in shorts and sandals you feel like his aunt teaching him about wine. He's nervous and boring and he drinks too much, but when you put your hand on his thigh and ask him about that massage, he does what he's told. In the morning, you text Janine with all the details. She doesn't text back after your run. She doesn't text back by the time you're off work. When you call it rings and rings until you get her voicemail.

You send: *Is something happening?*

And: *Is there anything I can do?*

You meet another man, then another. You meet so many, you forget their faces. Some return. Others don't. You make them rub your back. You make them tenderize you with massagers. You train them to take their time, running fingernails up your thighs until you forget your back ever hurt.

Running gets harder. Your back never stops being sore. You begin to notice jellyfish in your path when you run, shimmering in the night, the delicate ocean grace of their bodies useless on the shore. When you rest at sunrise, crabs linger at your feet, suddenly unafraid. Later, in the shower, you feel yourself washing off more than sand. You turn the hot water until the knob stops, letting the water cascade over all the parts of yourself you can't reach. The ache you used to relish is turning into something else, but you've never looked better. You look in the mirror and begin to notice an iridescence there. You open your bathrobe and let yourself see what's underneath. You raise an arm to the sun, fascinated by what catches in the light. There's a glitter there, just under your skin and it shines like a crystal in a stone, something shattered, buried and undeniable.

At night, you lay on your stomach to appease the pain in your back and listen to the steady pound of your heartbeat until your alarm goes off. When you stand up, your whole body cracks, like it's unaccustomed to being yours.

It's almost August when you see a chiropractor. He confirms what you've been feeling for weeks. When he says it, you finally let yourself admit it. You let yourself feel it.

"There's something wrong here." he says, and your relief surprises you.

"I've never seen anything like this." he says, and you feel somehow vindicated.

"How long have you had these?" he asks, running his hands over the twin knobs growing out of your back. You tell him and he makes a few urgent phone calls. He's sending you to a specialist. He's telling you to go today, they're expecting you. There's a terror in his eyes as he walks you into the lobby, pressing an address and a phone number into your palm.

"We're going to get you through this."

You go home and try to crack your back on your yoga ball, but the knobs get caught. At night, you can feel them pressing into you. You can feel them growing. It feels like they belong there.

A week passes. *Whatever you're doing, don't stop.* You begin your morning run earlier and earlier, 4 am, then 3. Until it's just you, pumping your legs alone in the night with only the skittering crabs to see you, lit by the pale of the moon and the dying shimmer of beached jellyfish. Knobs begin to form behind your calves. They appear at your forearm. The ones at your back grow flat and smooth, flexing up and down with the muscles of your back. You open the second to last jar of pale, pink cream and rub it onto yourself, paying careful attention to every knob and flap. Your skin is fully glowing now, a pale pink brilliance that pulses with the beat of your heart. You've never been more beautiful.

The chiropractor leaves one frantic voicemail, then another. So does your mother. So does Janice's ex-husband. So does yours. You don't listen to any of them. You listen instead to the crashing waves of the surf. You open the windows and fill the tub until it spills over, watching the water trickle and splash out the open door in a river you're meant to follow. You stay in the tub for hours watching your skin not prune, breathing in the euphoria of salted ocean air.

You wait for a very long time after the sun goes down. You open the last jar and coat yourself, head to toe, in layer after layer. When you're done, you lick your fingers clean and find that your hands are webbed. You think about Janice and hope the same thing happened to her, whe ever she is. You think about the little girl who waited for the ocean to rise and you realize that you're laughing. You walk into the living room, past your phone, past your laptop. You don't check your email. You don't check your messages. You stop for a moment and look at the calendar of crossed out squares and circled dates and wonder where the time went. On your way out the door, you think about what Janice said. *Whatever comes next.*

When you get to the beach, the crabs are waiting for you. There are hundreds of them, perfectly still. There's no place they'd rather scurry to. They part as you approach, glowing brilliant, pulsing in time with your racing heart. The waves beyond them pull and crash, pull and crash in time with your step. The ocean feels impatient to have you. You take one step and then another, flexing the fins on your back in the summer breeze until the water's over your bare feet, past the finlets behind your calves until you are fully submerged, ready to let yourself be the thing you've always been becoming.

When you say watch your mouth

Ami Patel

You need to know this: my mouth was forged
in another dimension. There, my mouth is heirloom
and harmonica, abundant with sea minerals and leaping
baby goats. But here, my mouth is pestilence. Root rot
and stillbirth. Here you insist my diagonal tooth,
the one that sprung early like an overeager ballerina,
makes me auspicious. My gums throb in the heat
of that lie. Do not offer a full plate of marigolds
while tunneling me in silence. Here, my mouth is decreed
renegade, as filmy as a Katrina duckling. Declared a target,
use caution and all weapons forged in the sneers of men.
Here, the corners of my mouth stay pinched together
like my legs. But in the bower of midnight, when you sleep,
my mouth screams in decibels heard only by those
with hips and ribs from other terrains, their demands
shredding the air like glitter: turn it up turn it up
Yes girl turn it up

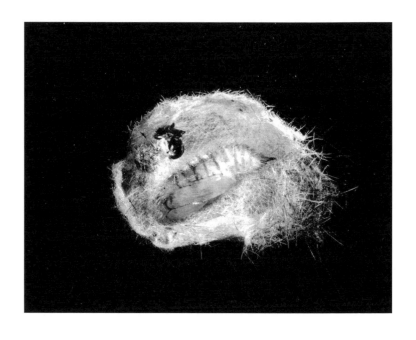

Douglas-fir tussock moth cocoon (Hemerocampa pseudotsugata).
Halfway, Oregon. 1959.

Wormholes

Alexis M Smith

When I was in college, I lived in a tiny apartment in the northwest part of town, near the trendy shops and restaurants. One night I woke up suddenly from a dream, full of dread. My bedroom window looked out onto a narrow, bricked courtyard where a single lamp post shone. For a while, I watched the door, where the shadows of two small japonicas, not quite in bloom, met in a troubling embrace. It was like one couldn't decide whether or not to strangle the other.

I had never been able to cope with the early hours after midnight.

I pushed back the covers and rose, searching the floor for my slippers. It was cold, and seemed colder in the dark, so I wrapped myself in a blanket. Twelve steps through the railroad flat and I was in the kitchen. Street lamps lit the room and my hand hovered over the light switch. I couldn't decide: there would be the tremendous shock to the senses when the light flooded the place, and then all the murkiness of everything at that hour, lit by the fluorescence.

I didn't turn on the light. The old refrigerator whimpered and sighed like a dreaming dog as I filled a glass by streetlight and turned to the window, to the narrow avenue crowded with apartments, the silvery glow on the trees and trash-tucked weeds.

As I raised the glass to my lips, there was a jarring knock on an apartment door just down the hall. Three firm knocks. I sputtered. Another human being, awake at that hour and steps away. I felt a jolt from some chamber of my heart. There was no safety in a knock on a door at that hour.

I set my glass on the counter and listened. Two breaths, three more knocks. It was the apartment across the hall and one down, occupied by another girl in her twenties, a hairdresser, who spent nights at her boyfriend's. Who would knock on her door at three in the morning? Then it occurred to me: how did the visitor get into the secured building? I hadn't heard the clatter of the entry, echoing up the stairwell; I hadn't heard the buzz of the door lock releasing. Was it another tenant? How did I not hear them come down the stairs, adjacent to my own door and constantly creaking with the arthritis of old buildings?

Three more knocks, louder and sharper than the last, impatient. I decided then that the hand must be small, the knuckles narrow peaks. The ball-peen hammer of a woman's fist.

I gathered the blanket around my shoulders and shuffled across the living room to the door. I heard the rustle of cloth, and imagined her arm dropping to her side. A faceless *she*, waiting for her knock to be answered, to be invited in. I tried to imagine how tall she was, her figure, the shape of her face, her hair color—anything to convince myself that there was nothing to worry about, but all I could venture was a spring jacket, something light and long—brushing the knees—like a trench coat, or what my mother would call a Mackintosh. Then came her footsteps and that same rustle of cloth toward my door. I flattened myself to it and held my breath. I wondered which way the footsteps would go: up to the second floor, or down the short flight to the entry. I would know, then, where she came from, where she was going. The feet fell consistently, firmly on the floorboards, until they reached my door. I reached defensively for the knob, and there was the slightest rattle when the weight of my hand fell on it. Abrupt silence followed. She had stopped. We were both listening.

Who are you afraid of? *You* are supposed to be here, I told myself. Who is this woman, stalking the halls of your building in the wee hours?

I pressed my ear to the door. The familiar creak of the stairs—up or down—never came. The door below did not clatter open or slam behind her. Though I thought I heard, once again, briefly, the airy movement of the Mackintosh (which by then I imagined was pale blue and dirty around the wrists, exactly like the one my mother owned). But after, my own pumping blood and unsteady breath were all I could hear.

I strained to hear her in the quiet for some time. Nothing. She must still be out there. No one could move so quietly in this building where we all knew when someone showered or cooked fish. Had she pulled off her shoes and crept silently to another floor? Was she waiting for me to look? Was she waiting for me to open the door? When I finally lifted my head to peer through the peephole, my breath snagged in my throat: the hall was empty.

I told my mother about the incident, some days later. I had been waking around three o'clock every morning since, imagining I heard the knocking again, but on my own door. It rattled me from dreams, and left a ringing in my head, but when I tip-toed to the door, it always rested quiet and cold in its frame. After a few days of this, I wasn't frightened. But in my normal waking hours I began to feel forlorn whenever I crossed the threshold of my apartment. I was sleep deprived, I told myself. After the long bus ride out to my mother's apartment in the suburbs, I was chattier than usual. I told her everything. I even told her about the Mackintosh.

"It was so strange," I said, nervous, "I imagined the girl wearing that old blue Mackintosh of yours—remember?—the one you bought in Scotland?"

She still had the coat, I was sure, she held onto everything. She bought the coat when she was my age, and had worn it all through my childhood, until her middle-aged body rejected it. She had been a celebrated scholar (she reminded me often) of archeology; she had unearthed a bog baby on the moors. Her very own bog baby, sacrificed (some said) centuries before and mummified in the peat. She was the envy of all the other scholars. It was rare to find a bog person at all, let alone a baby. When I was young she would tell the story of my birth in tandem with the story of the dig on the heath, the moment of her great discovery. She recalled the musk of leather and shit, and I never knew whether she was talking about me or the bog baby.

We were sitting across from each other at her kitchen table. I watched her for a reaction, but my mother's face always bore the same placidly disappointed look, as if the earth had offered up its final treasure to her years ago. "Where is my bog baby now?" this look of hers asked. She cocked her head.

"I didn't sleep at all after that," I finished, leaning back in my chair.

"Well," she said. Then she sighed and began picking dead leaves from the spider plants next to the window, all sprouting even more spider plants that she would eventually repot. There were spider plants in every window of the house, their grassy, variegated legs dangling over every surface, even the frosted tissue box of a window in the shower, where the shaggy creatures hoarded shampoo bottles. After an uncomfortable time had passed, she looked up.

"Louise Bourgeois was an insomniac and she sure got a lot done," she said, and stood to wash her coffee cup in the sink.

"I'm not an insomniac," I said, crushing a dried spindle of leaf to dust between my palms.

"Some people don't need sleep," she shrugged. She moved the sponge around the inside of the cup and stared through the houseplants in the kitchen window, out over the trimmed lawn of the complex and beyond, to the property line where the wilderness clawed at the landscaping. I could trace her thoughts as they delved the soil outside; I had heard some variation on the same time-space reverie before: ...*ice age, Missoula Flood, river basin, temperate coniferous rain forest, migratory hunter-gatherers, the winter villages of the Atfalati people, the lodges of the McKenzie fur traders, logging camps, the decimation of the Kalapuya tribes, European settlements, homesteads, farms, the removal of the remaining Indigenous population to Grand Ronde, and so on, till the suburban apartment complexes, strip malls, big box stores, and McMansions…* She rinsed her cup for a full minute, steam rising from the sink and her scalded hands.

I felt gratified that I had invoked this spell with the Mackintosh, then a jab of regret. My mother was no celebrated scholar now, not a professional or a professor. She worked with the elderly. Her clients were childless widows and spinsters with no one to look in on them. Women she referred to as "the Aunties." She visited a different Auntie five, sometimes six, days a week, including holidays. I was usually in-tow on Christmas and Thanksgiving, and even Valentine's Day. I learned how to hide my terror. Biologically they were human, but to my young eyes, they were the stuff of fairy tales. When they offered candy, I pocketed it and slipped it into the ashtray in the back seat of the car later. When they took my hand and smiled lovingly at me, I tried to love them back, if only so they wouldn't eat me.

Occasionally my mother would arrive after a few days to find one of the Aunties dead, gone sour and sunken like forgotten fruit. You always call the ambulance, no matter how obvious the expiration, and my mother said this was a damn shame. She wanted to dress them in nice things, from the backs of their closets, and put on their good shoes, like they were going out for their last, best game of bingo. She had a legal document, signed and notarized, that expressly demanded that I do as much with her fresh corpse. When I had asked her what I should dress her in she had said, "Oh, I won't care; I'll be long gone. Have fun with it."

I watched her at the sink, wondering if I should dress her in the Mackintosh when the time came.

She roused herself and put the cup in the drainer, turned off the water and wiped her hands on a towel. She picked a jam jar from the window sill and set it on the table in front of me. An adolescent spider plant bobbed in murky water.

"You should take a plant," she said, "I can't bring myself to kill the babies."

"They're not babies, Mom. It's asexual reproduction. They're clones. The same plant, over and over again."

My mother looked at me pityingly and shook her head.

She left the room, hunting tennis shoes for our walk around the man-made lagoon, where the blue herons were nesting again. I eyed the jar in front of me. Green slivers sprung from the lip. A skein of pale roots netted the glass, seeking a dark place.

I graduated from art school that summer. The recession was on, so I took the first job the temp agency offered me, at the American Biscuit Company. My alarm would go off at 2:30 in the morning, five days a week. I took a quick shower, put in my ear buds and rode my bike north to the peninsula at the delta of the city's two rivers. Factories, steel fabricators, and petroleum depots hemmed the houses and schools and parks within. Viewed from above, the peninsula looked like a singed, quilted oven mitt. American Biscuit was the biggest bakery in the city, baking off and packaging popular national brands like Etiquette Crackers and Counter Top Cupcakes. On dry days, when the winds blew from the northwest, neighborhoods four miles away smelled like muffins. I started on the packaging line, making decent money for temp work. Two years later I was first shift supervisor of the Oven.

I never hated it, despite my mother's increasing bafflement. My friends tended bars and waited tables and worked at record stores. Those were acceptable jobs for Bachelors of Arts—or even Masters of Arts. Their tattoos and dyed hair were their uniforms. I wore a papery white coat and booties; I came home dusted with a fine, sweet powder. I belonged in a nursery rhyme.

"You should see the cupcakes," I told her, "all lined up in the packaging line every day like a Damien Hirst. Chocolate, strawberry, yellow; chocolate, strawberry, yellow."

"'Yellow' isn't a flavor," she said.

"'Yellow' is a flavor," I told her. "It's Flavor 79-A2. I'm not supposed to know, but it's mostly vanillin and limonene."

"You smell like marshmallows," she complained.

The aroma never left my hair or my skin, no matter what kind of soap I used.

My mother told me I would be an artist when I was very small. It was a dream, planted in her head the day she realized her cycle had stopped, and there were clusters of cells becoming human-shaped inside her. Merle Boleyn, the surrealist painter and writer, was a visiting lecturer at the University that year, and she wanted to see "the fen girl," my mother's discovery. After three quarters of an hour staring at the tanned, dehydrated babe from all sides, her long silver hair draped around her, Boleyn turned to my mother with tears in her eyes. "A leanbh mo chroí," she whispered, *child of my heart*, "every womb is a wormhole."

She was seventy-seven, and my mother was twenty-four. They never met again, but my mother felt a tug inside—buried between the heart and the navel—a drawing outward, whenever she thought of what Boleyn said to her. She sought out Boleyn's work and studied it, took notes in a cloth-bound journal which she read to me after I was born, like a book of fairy tales. Boleyn wrote a treatise on reincarnation. She recited poems in dead languages to blindfolded audiences. She painted portraits of herself through the centuries, in historic dress, being tortured, beheaded, and burned at the stake, then birthed again by future iterations of herself. My mother the scholar would soon give birth to me, and in doing so, she would become another version of herself.

As for the *facts* of my conception, my mother treated me as if I were the natural outcome of a liberated young woman traveling abroad in the 1970's. My paternity cast aside, it was the story of Merle Boleyn I knew by heart, as if she had brought about my existence, like a witch with whom my mother had struck a bargain. After their fateful encounter, I slipped through the wormhole into this world from god knows where. From the darkness. From the bog.

"But where will you paint?" my mother would fret, standing in one of my efficiency kitchens, in one of my dioramas of an apartment. There was exasperation in her voice, and despair—fear, even—as if, after all, the bargain would not be kept.

One night my mother called me as I biked home from a party. I stopped at the curb near a Catholic church to answer. One of the Aunties had died the previous month, and she had gone to help her nieces—her actual kin—clean out the house. She did all the unpleasant jobs: the old panty sorting, and the garbage can scrubbing, and the hauling to the thrift store, while the middle-aged nieces from California had pecked and squawked at each other like gulls over the few precious tidbits. That night my mother had stayed late to clean in silence while the nieces went out for dinner.

"I *found* something," she told me, an echo of the young archeologist in her voice. "Where are you? Come over."

When I rolled up to the little saltbox, it was familiar to me, though I had never met this particular Auntie. Small and tidy and contained, windows lit; the lawn was knee-high and aglow with fallen maple blossoms, like an Easter basket full of candy.

I hopped off my bike and carried it onto the porch. My mother opened the door abruptly and ushered me in.

"Hurry," she said, "Before they get back."

She took my wrist softly in her hand and led me down the hall to the dead Auntie's bedroom. In the closet was a trap door to a narrow attic under the eaves, barely more than a crawl space. I climbed up on a chair after my mother, then onto the short, creaky ladder rigged to the door. The floorboards were warped planks laid over the ceiling beams that rocked side to side with our weight. I sneezed twice before my eyes adjusted to the flashlight pointed at the far side of the space. There was something in the corner gleaming through the darkness and dust. My mother skittered over as quickly as she could and squatted there.

"Over here. Come on," she beckoned.

I tipped myself forward to avoid the slope of roof and joined her.

"What is it?"

I squatted precariously on the weft of a plank. It was a half-gallon jar, full of amber liquid, frothy at the top, like beer. My mother had picked it up, I could tell, because her fingerprints were all over the layer of dust on it. She reached out and shook it. Something bobbed through the soup toward the glass.

"There's something in there," I said, reaching out to brush more dust from the jar. It looked like a biological specimen, an organ. My mother lifted the jar to my face. The organ teetered and effervesced in the murk. It looked like a misshapen heart with two rangy arms, outstretched.

"It's a heart?" I asked.

My mother scoffed. "It's a uterus."

Then she laughed with such mirth—more than I thought she had in her.

Downstairs Mom made tea. She showed me a portrait of the dead Auntie when she was a girl, in the nineteen-thirties, all white lace and bows like a child bride—*First Communion*—Mom sneered. Then snapshots at my age, in the Fifties, bushy eyebrows and rhinestone glasses that came back in vogue briefly when I was in high school. Mom was carefully stowing all the memorabilia into labeled shoe boxes for the nieces. We sipped our tea, the pictures spread out on the table.

"In ancient Greece," Mom said, "they believed that the uterus could move throughout a woman's body, wreaking havoc on all the body's systems. The 'wandering uterus,' they called it. Pregnancy was the cure. A hysterectomy was a death sentence."

"I've read Freud, Mom. I just don't understand why she kept it."

She rose to throw her tea bag in the trash.

"Some things become more terrifying when you try to forget them," she said.

The next week I signed a rental agreement with the nieces. They returned to California to wait out the recession and the lousy housing market. I promised them I would keep the flowerbeds weeded and scrape off the peeling wall paper, put up fresh coats of paint. We watched them drive away in their rental, then began unloading Mom's station wagon full of my things. Inside, Mom brought out a few boxes of things she had pretended to donate (in case the nieces threw a fit): tea towels and vases and a frayed paperback called *The Cookbook for Poor Poets & Others* by Ann Rogers. She put all of these things back in the drawers and cupboards they had lived in before.

"A place for everything and everything in its place," she said, winking at me.

I looked at her saucer-eyed and we both laughed. The uterus was still in the attic, tucked away by the chimney.

We were giddy together for the first time in decades. Like when I was much younger and one of the Aunties would give me a suitcase or shopping bag full of her old clothes for dress-up. Mom would make us cups of strong Scottish tea with milk and sugar, and we would go through the clothes deliberately, one piece at a time. I tried on everything, however large or grotesque. Sometimes the Aunties gave me slips and braziers and nylons with holes in the crotch; sometimes they gave me costume jewelry in violet pastille tins, and nubs of ancient, waxy lipstick. Mom would stand behind me before the tall mirror at the end of the hall as we looked at my small body in the Aunties' clothes. She would toss her head back and laugh low and long, her eyes full of tears.

I picked up the cookbook and thumbed through a few pages. There were specks of béchamel sauce on the page for Welsh rarebit, smudges of the Auntie's fingerprints.

"Was she a poet?" I asked, looking up at my mother balanced on a step stool to hang a spider plant in the kitchen window.

"Hm?"

"Auntie Ramona. Was she a poet?"

"Oh, maybe in spirit. She answered phones for Daimler for fifty years." She climbed down and eyed the plant, swaying over the sink. "She was lonely, anyway," she said, plucking a dead leaf.

Weary, Mom drove home late. She was spry, but fraying at the edges, beginning to show signs I had watched her watching in the Aunties. I kissed her at the door and made sure she turned on her headlights. I caught my own reflection in all the dark windows as I walked through the house.

I half-brushed my teeth, made the bed and crawled between the sheets in my underwear. Even my old bed felt bigger, my feet stretching towards the corners I couldn't reach. I tried sleeping, but I couldn't reset my internal clock. It measured time, just like other clocks, but the sun and the moon were in opposite positions. My eyelids drifted up whenever I lowered them. I stared around the room. The opened boxes heaped around my bed looked like a family of animals. Bears, maybe. Mama bear, baby bear, baby bear.

I wondered whether wild animals ate the uteruses of their prey, and whether they savored it, like one might a heart, or whether they gorged on the uterus ravenously along with all the other tender bits? Or maybe they saved it. Maybe they left it behind as an offering, like our cats did the bloody pebbles of mouse organs on our doorstep?

I reached for the lamp, and a notebook and pen from my bedside drawer. I propped myself up and drew the she-bear and her babies until morning. Cloudy, weak light and generic birdsong lulled me to sleep.

I went on like this for some time—about a year—living in the Auntie's salt-box, waking at 2:30 A.M. and biking to work at the bakery, staying up on my nights off to draw until morning. More and more drawings every day, and then I painted. Always landscapes with animals and women, sometimes dancing, sometimes eating each other. And then I painted the scenes on the walls, until I was surrounded by a wilderness. A deep green summer of wilderness, a wilderness with no hibernation.

Then one day I woke to a knocking at my door. It threw me from a vacant sleep, ringing in my ears. I looked around the room and listened for the quiet neighborhood, all the workers still working, the wind in the trees outside the open window. I felt the chill of recent rain and heard the knocking again. I said to myself, *mail carrier*, and then, looking at the clock, realizing the mail usually comes late morning: *Mormon, environmentalists, Girl Scouts.* And as I lay there, adrenaline draining away, willing them to go away, the knock came again, familiar this time. *The Mackintosh.* I threw back the blankets, and ran down the hall to the door—warm feet on cold wood, heavy-headed—and halted in the living room. Would she knock again? That insistent *clockclockclock.* I crept to the door and put my ear up to it. I had no peephole, and no reliable window from which to peek without sticking my whole head out. I heard the movement of cloth, shifting weight on the boards of the porch. Then a hand on the doorknob, testing the latch, the shudder of its weight in my palm.

"Who's there?!" I screamed, voice cracking. Silence. No reply, only a flutter, and a persistent drip as the tension on the knob released. In a flood of panic and courage—she couldn't slip away, not again—I yanked open the door.

The sudden glare off the wet street blinded me. Behind my eyelids I saw the ragged outline of myself, a bright white-eyed face with an open, gaping mouth, a topaz aura sinking into an murky abyss, the hot ammonia of her breath on my cheeks. I opened my eyes. Of course she was gone. Only a filthy puddle at my feet.

On Mother's Day I stayed awake all night and into the morning, then I took the bus out to my mother's townhouse for brunch. I brought my notebook full of she-bears, wrapped in brown paper and ribbon. The weeping began before she opened it. I stood behind her at the table, to see what she saw. She sniffled and I pulled a crooked dried leaf from her tangled gray curls. She lingered over each drawing, turning the pages carefully, slowly. As she progressed through the notebook, her tears dried. She inhaled each breath though her mouth and held it, then exhaled short, raspy sighs through her nose. I couldn't see her face or her expression. Finally she spoke.

"They're eating... hearts?" she asked, bewildered, not looking at me.

I leaned over to see her face, a yawning ache in my chest. Her brow was furrowed; she didn't remember our night in the attic, her final discovery. She had been forgetting lots of things like this, moments we shared, and probably ones we didn't, ones that preceded me, dark apertures where her life should be. Wormholes. Later, I would sneak into her bedoom while she brushed her hair and teeth; I would make sure the Mackintosh was still there; I would pull it over my shoulders and feels its weight, slip my hands into the empty pockets, then return it to the hanger at the back of the closet.

"Yes, Ma," I said, smoothing her hair. "Hearts."

Douglas-fir tussock moth rearing cages, Sellwood Lab.
Portland, Oregon. 1965.

Digital Autobiography

Bethan Tyler

*"Nothing I know matters more
than what never happened"*

—"Hearsay," John Burnside

I.
Wherever I sleep, there's always
someone rummaging through the bins
at dawn: a fox, a raccoon, a person
after the after-effects of my life,
My corks & my crumbs, my cotton balls
slick with skin cells & glycolic acid.
I don't mind. I leave the blinds open
while I dress, I tell the Internet all
my best stories. I'm just being pragmatic:
Bezos owns my life anyway. Data,
he calls it, as though a soul can be reduced
to strings of binary. I'll have the last laugh,
I'll let the corks & crumbs, like tea leaves,
dictate my impossible future. I'll write
narratives & anti-narratives, let the foxes
pick the right conclusion.

II.

When I was born, the stars arranged themselves
accordingly. Call it astrology, call it magic, but
I was born under Pisces, to the music of foxes &
a cheap CD of Crowded House my mother
preferred to an epidural. Or call it data,
call me grooves on a CD, ready to be played.
I don't mind. I still believe in small magic, in
happenstance & surprise. Bezos knows this, too,
sells me acids, incense, books of poetry. But
poems make new worlds, so let this be
my incantation. Let this be my
fragmentation. I won't let you write me
in ones and zeros. I was born under Pisces,
to a pair of foxes making music in the bins.
I'll be a perfect string of twos.

Kate Lebo in conversation with Alayna Becker

Spring 2021 · Digital Exchange

I first met Kate Lebo in 2014 when she first moved to Spokane, Washington and I was on my way out. Lebo is a thoughtful weaver of narratives and a deft craftsperson in writing and in the domestic. We met in our own internet void to discuss these topics and her book, *The Book of Difficult Fruit: Arguments for the Tart, Tender, And Unruly* which came out April 2021.

    Kate Lebo's first collection of nonfiction, *The Book of Difficult Fruit: Arguments for the Tart, Tender, and Unruly*, was published by FSG in April 2021. She's the author of the cookbook *Pie School* and the poetry chapbook *Seven Prayers to Cathy McMorris Rodgers*, and is the coeditor, with Samuel Ligon, of *Pie & Whiskey: Writers Under the Influence of Butter and Booze*. She lives in Spokane, Washington, where she is an apprentice cheesemaker to Lora Lea Misterly of Quillisascut Farm.

Becker

Hey Kate! I'm so glad you're here! Let's start with a definition. What is a difficult fruit?

Lebo

At first it was a fruit that defied my expectations of sweetness and ease. Raw quince smells great, tastes terrible, and doesn't yield its pleasures until cooked.

Wheat flour is the basis of beloved breads and cakes and pies, but wheatberry dust is explosive and flour makes some people sick. As I wrote more of the book, different types of difficulty arose. The way almond flavor and cyanide coexist in the kernel of stone fruits. How some blackberry vines are invasive. A bounty of plums can become a chore and a mess. And then there's the way each fruit's difficulty can become metaphors for human difficulty—the failure of our bodies, the fragility of our relationships, the magical thinking we use to identify what will heal us, and the way nurturing and harm can get all tangled up. Whoever said we're not supposed to anthropomorphize plants and animals will hate my book. I stopped listening to that criticism—or truism, or whatever it is. I hear it echo faintly in a round with "kill your darlings" and "show don't tell."

Becker

One of the many things I love about you is your claim on "domestic artist", which is an idea I identify with, but was afraid to claim until you did.

Lebo

This line in the Faceclock chapter really stands out to me, "Yet sometimes I can look at my life, which I have lived as a certain kind of feminist and a certain kind of artist, and I see another woman who's struggling to make her peace with being at home." I'd love to hear more about your thoughts on this struggle, especially in the face of your mother's refrain in the Kiwifruit chapter, "I didn't get enough done."

I've been rereading Naben Ruthnum's book Curry: Eating, Reading, and Race for a nonfiction class I'm teaching, and I just reencountered this great line: "Reading, eating, and remembering are all activities that begin domestically." It's such a clear, concise reminder that literary impulses develop in the same place that culinary impulses do, that home is the place we begin—and where some of us sustain—a life of the mind. A reminder like this shocks me every time I see it. Home life and artistic life coexist. It's that simple. And it's not. On one hand, the invisible domestic labor that occurs at home is not valued publicly with money or status or whatever. On the other, laboring within the home is private, quiet, so deeply personal. It's an expression of one's inner life, and a way to protect it. I'm talking about sweeping the floor. But I'm also talking about writing poems.

There's something to be said here about the story my family tells itself about productivity and self worth. I don't think I can say it directly. I'll try to say it this way:

Every day, like everyone else, I have a limited number of hours within which to do meaningful work. Even on days when the work I do really is meaningful, I might not know it, or I won't complete it. That creates an unending sense of being stuck under a pile of my own making. The pressure of that pile helps me get anything done in the first place—nothing like three blown deadlines to help me turn one thing in on time. In the meantime, I'm weaving domestic tasks that have nothing to do with paid work or artistic work into whatever breaks I have given myself. I do dishes, I weed the garden, I throw out junkmail, I prep dinner, I flip my cheese. These tasks feel like a way to control my ever-avalanching to-do pile. They are also tasks I turn to when procrastinating, or when too wound around my own axle to think straight on a piece of writing. Usually they do not feel like worthy uses of my time. I tell myself it doesn't matter if they are worthy. And so, by the end of the day, I talk myself into a truce: I didn't get enough done, but that's okay. Time to rest.

I had a baby last October, and part of the reset of that experience has been that sometimes I realize all these deadlines I've been trying to hit for the last 15, 20 years—I made them up! I can unmake them! I can just hang out with the baby and forget all these made up deadlines! It's been lovely and disconcerting. We'll see how long this mood lasts.

Your question makes me think of something Syliva Plath wrote in her diary about the ideal life with Ted Hughes being one of "books, babies, and beef stews." The book of literary criticism I read that quote in made a big deal about the parataxis of her phrase. The critic thought this indicated that those three things, to Plath, were equally important. That phrase felt like permission and recognition. Wanting to write books, to be in a deep love relationship with another artist, to have a family, to cook, none of these are anathema to making art. I didn't have to listen to people who said that artistic output occurs in inverse proportion to domestic labor. Or that, as a woman, I could be an artist or have a family, but not both. (Do people still say that? Has that changed? It seems like it has. When I look around my community in Spokane, I'm surrounded by writers who are parents).

Calling myself a domestic artist is a joke and not a joke. It feels like a fast, winky way to express the line I walk by being an artist who enjoys domestic arts. Domestic arts aren't Art—cooking a stew is not writing a poem—but they are a deep, traditional, everyday creative practice. For a long time I felt silly that I loved doing the stereotypical woman thing—baking pies, all that. When we were taking my portrait for Pie School, I refused to wear a full apron because I thought it was a subservient garment. In my everyday life, full aprons are practical and necessary as hell.

I get and give so much joy with my work in food, but that labor can turn on a dime depending on how the gift of that labor is received and regarded. I used to worry a lot that by making pies and writing cookbooks, no one would take me seriously as a writer of anything else. That, to someone who doesn't know any better, I might look like a housewife. I don't worry about that anymore.

Becker

You're a writer who works just as deftly in research as in poetic description. I feel so much of your own becoming as a person and an artist in these pages.

From plums and leaving a relationship you'd outgrown, to finding maternal separation like Persephone and pomegranates. The fruit of this book is also a personal transformation over time. What kind of awareness did you have of that aspect while writing, and which portions did you find on the page?

Lebo

I knew when I started writing this book that I'd discover what it was about as I wrote. I figured (I hoped!) that writing this book would transform me into a better writer. I didn't know that it would chart personal transformations too. I believe the best essays are written with a sense of not-knowing and discovery. That if an essay ends up being about what I thought it was about, I've failed. I had to trust that a structure, thematic arcs, character development, an argument—all the things that hold a book together and make it bigger than its parts—would develop as I wrote. The not-knowing was scary. I was stuck so many times. Many of my chapters are the result of coming unstuck somehow, through research or cooking or a joke my husband Sam made, or a read he gave me on a draft. Sometimes I would read my drafts aloud and send recordings of them to Maya Jewell Zeller, who, like Sam, is an incredible writer and editor. She'd listen to them on her commute from Spokane to Ellensburg, where she teaches at Central Washington University, then call and leave a message to tell me what I was writing about. May we all have partners and friends who can read us so well!

This book took seven years to write, so I wonder if the transformation you describe is also a consequence of time passing. If I couldn't help but encode transformation within the pages because I came back to them so many times over so many years. The self that started this book isn't who I am now.

Becker

One thing I know for sure about you is your dedication to process. I remember you once telling me you needed to spend six years on a jam recipe before you could be sure you were done. When I heard that I was like, who has six years? But Kate Lebo does. It's clear to me by the construction of this book that you make that same commitment to process in your writing.

Domestic labor and writing craft are both invisible. The whole purpose of craft is to give shape to the piece from behind just as domestic labor is best when the labor behind it is tucked away. How did you approach the construction of this book?

Lebo

Ha! Did I say that? I meant it. And I was exaggerating. Recipe development doesn't have to take that long. But I do prefer to have years of practice and mistakes under my belt before writing a recipe. I'm doing that with cheese now. Making so many mistakes. Keep in mind those six years happen while everything else is happening—I'm making the jam anyway because it's fun, not because I intend to write a recipe about it. Then, one day, I can write a recipe, and if I have a book project like this to fit it in, I do.

As far as constructing this book goes, it began with the title. I spent some time wondering what a difficult fruit might be. I tried to imagine if there was a way to turn a wheat dust explosion in 1878 into a metaphor for a breakup, or a taste of astringent quince into a metaphor for craving knowledge about missing family members. Early on I decided the book would be an abecedarian. I chose this form in part because the arbitrary limit of the alphabet helped me stop flailing around in my writing, and in part because I love the expansive lie of the encyclopedia—that within its alphabet, it contains everything. I love the way an alphabetized book on fruit like Nigel Slater's Ripe makes me feel like I'm entering someone's secret garden.

At the time I began writing *The Book of Difficult Fruit*, I admired books written in a collage style very much. I still do. I wanted to write one myself, and I tried that style for the first five essays. I liked how the associative leaps of collage made it easier to contain contradiction and relieved me, for the most part, from constructing a straightforward argument. I even numbered my sections à la *Bluets*. Jenna Johnson, my editor at FSG, did away with the numbers immediately, which was the right choice. It felt like she'd removed the scaffolding. Beneath the ways I was imitating books I admired, I started to find a form that suited me and the book better.

What remains of the collage form is a weave of many ways of knowing. In this book, scientific, ethnobotanical, and historical research coexists with memoir, which coexists with an amateur's gathering of empirical evidence and all my successes or failures to procure, cook, and eat difficult fruits. I interview culture bearers and farmers and gardeners. Literary and biblical references coexist with quotes from the famous witchbook of the Pennsylvania Dutch and herbals like Culpeper's and Grieve's. When it came to research, I tried to be omnivorous.

Becker

Each fruit stands on its own, but the memoir continues throughout. How did you approach closing and opening narrative arcs across essays?

Lebo

Through failure. Opening arcs is easy. Developing them was easy. Figuring out how to bring them to a satisfying close without tying them up too neatly or forcing some sort of thesis or purpose or lesson learned—that was hard. Frankly, most of the arcs here, I didn't intentionally close. They just sort of found a good resting place as I wrote the final chapters. I was afraid the whole time that I wouldn't nail the dismount, especially since I didn't have an outline or a plan for the book, I just tried to see one step ahead of myself. Despite that anxiety, I had faith that something would arise within each chapter that helped tie it up, or lay it to rest, or whatever metaphor I'm mixing here. I can't really tell you how I did it. I can tell you that it didn't work for a long time, and then it did. And that the book went through three major drafts.

Becker

One of the outlier essays, to me anyway, is Juniper Berry. This essay is about you supporting your friend during her abortion and begins, "This is none my business and not my story," Juniper berry, as you note, is an abortificant. Can you talk about why abortion and fruit as medicine was important to you to dicuss in this book?

Lebo

Early in my research for this book, I visited the Miller Library at UW, where I did a fairly unfocused search and grab of everything I could find on ume, medlar, gooseberries, and juniper. I'd start with each book's index and read everything that mentioned whatever fruit I was focusing on. Juniper caught my attention early because the index in Gabrielle Hamilton's *Encyclopedia of Folk Medicine* cross-references it with abortion, but elsewhere, my juniper sources didn't mention that association. This sort of thing continued— I could find references to juniper being used as an abortifacient, but no details, no recipes, nothing really substantive or trustworthy. My friend Kathryn Neurnberger was working on her great book *The Witch of Eye* at the time, and had just published Rue, a book of poems about herbs historically used as birth control. She clarified my confusion by letting me in on an open secret: historical methods of birth control are usually obfuscated and lied about. If I couldn't find details, that was to be expected.

Which reminded me of the complete mystery that surrounds the death of my grandfather's mother, who maybe died from measles or maybe died from a botched abortion, we'll never know, but once again the taboo on talking about this and on giving women control over their fertility means I'm never going to know. Like most of the rest of us, I have to live with rumor.

Which led me to think about the modern experience of abortion. If I was going to tell the story of helping my friend through terminating her pregnancy, I needed to strike a very delicate balance. In this story of a very ordinary but very complicated decision, how would I preserve my friend's privacy while plumbing the historical complexities of her choice?

Which brought me to the question of whether or not it is "okay" for me to tell a personal story about a loved one when their lives intersect with mine. That's something I struggled with through the whole book. I mean, my poor mother! The story I tell in "Juniper Berry," about holding my friend's hand—we worked together on that to decide what to show and what to keep private. My friend was incredibly generous and vulnerable with her story. I'm so grateful. That chapter and that discussion wouldn't be what it is without her at the heart of it. The process of figuring out what she could bear me telling, and what she could not bear—that feels related to the secrets of herbal birth control, too. My friend needed privacy because her decision was very personal, but she needed privacy also because she did not want to bear the judgement of others. The secret part of that story protects her, as the secrecy around historical methods of birth control protected women who administered or used them. But it also breaks the chain of story about this very normal choice, these very normal medicines. It contributes to the taboo. I couldn't figure out a way around this paradox. Within the essay, that felt fitting.

Becker

The question of abortion is so central to the domestic. Abortion is central to home health. It's incredible, as you note in this essay, the way this aspect of the archive became so eroded over time that it hardly exists at all. I was so shocked to read that your great grandmother lost her life to unsafe abortion, because my great great grandmother also died that way, orphaning my great grandfather, which has affected every proceeding generation of my family.

Abortion is treated as a difficult fruit, but as we know, it doesn't have to be. Abortion is normal, and no matter what the Supreme Court has to say, home abortion, as this important chapter proves, has been happening forever, and will continue to happen. As more abortion bans go into effect across our country, I so appreciate you bringing the vestiges of our history of managing health at home to light.

One of my favorite things about this book is that it isn't an argument for or against difficult fruits, it's a book that takes the reader by the hand and says, look, taste, smell, consume. This book says fruit isn't simple, or made just for you, it is complex and vexed with difficult realities.

Just as suffering is central to the human condition, but it is not inextricable from joy or goodness or whatever. Difficult fruits contain the suffering and the joy. How did the process of rendering all of these difficult fruits, literally and metaphorically, shift your view on them?

Lebo

The quick answer, the one I've found from talking about this book for a couple months now, is that engaging with the difficulty of a supposedly sweet thing has helped me have a more authentic relationship with it, one that contains the dark and the light. For me, when I write about food, it's always about my relationship with people and art. By trying to engage with the difficulty of fruit, I found a way into thorny questions that I wouldn't have been able to ask myself or others if I'd come at them head-on.

I remember, during the years of writing this book, being able to concentrate on the peculiarities and difficulties of each fruit, the pleasure that gave me (I'm one of those freaks who loves small, repetitive tasks), the attention I could give and the attention each fruit demanded of me. I couldn't just unwrap it like a banana and shove it in my face. I appreciate how difficulty required attention, and how attention gave me pleasure and quiet, and how the challenge of trying to figure out ways to procure a difficult fruit or prepare a difficult fruit or make a difficult fruit delicious, all the failure and dead ends and frustrations, exposed me to all sorts of happy accidents. Medar, for example, just doesn't taste very good to me unless it's jelly, and then it tastes divine, but the process I took to figure that out highlighted all the food-forms we use to preserve fruit. I started thinking of these forms like they were a family tree: jelly, jam, pickles, conserves, extracts, brandies, fruit leathers, ferments, shrubs, cordials, ice creams, condiments, I could go on (I go on).

There's another answer about my relationship outside of books to fruit. I would have been able to tell you this answer before my son was born, but now I can't remember it. Talk about transformation! Now what I'd say is, I miss my difficult fruits! Preserving fruit doesn't fit in life with an infant. Jam is molten and can scorch in a second. The chances of injury or failure are just too high. Cheesemaking, however, works well, so for the time being I've channeled all my preserving energies into milk.

Becker

This book, of course, required so much labor. Cooking is so much labor. Cleaning. I think about Italian Plum and W. I definitely related to this sense of implied labor in relationships with men before and I felt this sick sense of accomplishment from it. How did you, as an artist and as a person, claim your labor for your internal and artistic work?

Lebo

Therapy, baby.

Becker

Ok, speaking of cleaning, having been in your sweet little kitchen once, it seems like you've got to be constantly doing dishes to keep up with your research. Who is doing all these dishes?

Sam, of course! Haha. Both of us. I do my recipe-testing dishes but then I often poop out and he's left with our actual dishes, which he does without complaining because he's a saint. Now that we have Cy, if we don't both do dishes constantly we are buried under food and filth, so there's no more abandoning that chore to Sam. We're in this sink together.

Becker

Love that so hard! I was certain you were just like, throwing away pans and starting over. What a guy.

So I wanna get down and dirty with what really matters: grocery stores. What's your fantasy grocery store line up across the PNW? Farmers markets count.

Lebo

My favorite grocery store is probably Lora Lea Misterly's pantry at Quillisascut Farm (she's my cheesemaking mentor through the Washington Center for Cultural Traditions). She makes incredible preserves of all kinds, and all kinds of cheeses, and sometimes there's polenta to buy, or hot sauce, or extra eggplants, or apricot pits, or green walnuts to turn into Nocino. I've visited her during every season now, and every month there's something new to discover and enjoy, and it's all so fresh.

If we could have some kind of combo Perry Street Market/Vinegar Flats Farm CSA/Uwajimaya/fancy but affordable wine store/cheese shop/Culture Bread-mart—oh, I'd cook myself to heaven. I guess in Spokane we sort of do have that! The LINC Co-op sells a lot of this stuff, plus spices and Palouse-grown pulses and and and...

Becker

Wow, what a hot lineup.

To me, Spokane is the definition of a difficult fruit. Sweet with a dark past, approachable, but thick skinned, and certainly rotten in parts. If Spokane was a difficult fruit, which would she be?

Lebo

Hmm... Spokane might be most like durian, a fruit that would never, ever grow here. Not universally loved, but heartily defended by those who do know and love it. Incomprehensible to someone who has no firsthand experience of it, but has heard enough to be of the opinion they don't like it. Worth the effort to acquire the taste. Covered in a tough, prickly rind that, when hacked through, reveals a soft heart. Like nothing else.

Canyon City fire, Malheur National Forest, Oregon. 1937.

Blend, clay, coffee

Gwendolyn Morgan

Brimmed coffee cup, teal flowers on red clay
the beans come from Guatemala
coffee, light roast
the poinsettias bloom on other holidays
white salt on white of egg
white of eye, pupil, retina
she struggles to find her way out of
glaucoma, macular degeneration
loss of vision and determination
loss of freedom and independence
metastatic cancer, mets blocking reason
COVID-19 pneumonia receding
she chooses a feeding tube, a j-peg
not an image from a photograph
yet a circular loop of plastic
that takes white artificial nutrition directly
to the stomach, the axis mundi
the center of the thought, the flower.

Now she begins to hold
the cup in her trembling hands.

Contributors.

Cari Luna *(Safe)* is the author of *The Revolution of Every Day*, which won the Ken Kesey Award for Fiction. A fellow of Yaddo and Ragdale, her writing has appeared in *The Nation, Guernica, Salon, Jacobin, Electric Literature, Catapult, PANK,* and elsewhere. She lives in Portland, Oregon.

Kaitlyn Airy (she/her) *(My Body Is The House I Haunt)* was raised on a small island in the Salish Sea. A Korean American poet and fiction writer, her work appears or is forthcoming in *Ecotheo, Crab Creek Review, Post Road,* and *Cream City Review.* In 2020, she won the Phyllis L Ennes contest, hosted by the Skagit River Poetry Foundation. She is an MFA candidate in poetry at the University of Virginia.

Rachel Brown (*Peaches* and *Above the Hearth*) holds Bachelor's degrees in Creative Writing and English Literature, as well as Master's degree in English Literature from Central Washington University, where she also taught composition. Her creative work appears in *Northwest Boulevard* and *Okay Donkey.* She is currently reading, writing, and running in Eastern Washington.

Lisa Chen *(Hoarding Secrets)* is a Taiwanese American writer based on Duwamish Territory/Seattle, Washington. By day she works on environmental justice policies and by night (and very early morning), she writes on themes of generational grief, inherited loneliness, and food as living memories. She is a contributing editor at *The Seventh Wave.*

Patrycja Humienik *(coping mechanisms* and *How will you begin?)* is a Polish-American writer and movement artist based in Seattle, WA. Her poetry is featured/forthcoming in *Passages North, Four Way Review, Hobart, The Boiler, The Shallow Ends*, and *Sporklet*, among others. She serves as assistant poetry editor for *Newfound* and events director for *The Seventh Wave*. Find Patrycja on twitter @jej_sen.

Katie Lee Ellison *(Woven at the Center)* has been a Hugo House Fellow, a fellow at the Yiddish Book Center, and a 2020 Tin House Summer Workshop attendee. She's been working for a very long time on a memoir tentatively titled *Everything We Wanted*, pieces of which are published in *Shenandoah, Crab Creek Review, Arcadia*, and elsewhere. She holds a BA in English Lit from Wellesley College and an MFA from the University of Idaho.

Kate Garcia *(Car Camping Outside Livingston, MT)* is poet and waitress from Southern California. She spent six years loving and crying and eating in Portland, Oregon before heading to Missoula as an MFA candidate at the University of Montana.

Jaton Rash *($23.00 A Night)* has been published in *The Portland Alliance* and *Yoga Northwest Magazine*. His lifelong passions include writing, cycling and yoga. He works for Portland Public Schools and has lived in the Portland, Oregon area for over thirty years.

Phillip Barron *(Displacement Activities)* teaches at Lewis & Clark College in Portland, Oregon while writing a dissertation in philosophy for a PhD from the University of Connecticut. His first book of poetry, *What Comes from a Thing* (Fourteen Hills Press, 2015) won the Nicolás Guillén Outstanding Book Award for philosophical literature, and his poems have been featured in many national journals.

Erin Pringle *(Chair $75 OBO)* is the author of a novel, *Hezada! I Miss You,* and two short story collections, *The Whole World at Once* and *The Floating Order*. She has written three chapbooks: *How The Sun Burns Among Hills of Rock and Pebble*; *The Lightning Tree*; and *The Wandering House*. Her work has been selected as a Best American Notable Non-Required Reading and performed in L.A.'s New Short Fiction Series. A recipient of a Washington State 2012 Artist Trust Fellowship, she lives in Washington State with her partner, Heather, and son, Henry.

Nicholas Bradley *(Clouds Taken for Mountains)* is a Canadian poet, literary critic, and editor. His most recent book, *Rain Shadow*, was published by the University of Alberta Press in 2018. He lives in Victoria, British Columbia.

Soramimi Hanarejima *(A Certain Brightness)* is the author of *Visits to the Confabulatorium*, a fanciful story collection Jack Cheng said, "captures moonlight in Ziploc bags, and gives us the pleasure of opening them, one by one." Visit her at CognitiveCollage.net.

Rena Priest *(The Ballad of Aunt Lottie)* is a Poet and an enrolled member of the Lhaq'temish (Lummi) Nation. She has been appointed to serve as Washington State's Poet Laureate for the term of April 2021-2023. She is the recipient of the Vadon Foundation Fellowship (2020), and an Allied Arts Foundation Professional Poets Award (2020). She has attended residencies at Hedgebrook, Mineral School, and Hawthornden Castle. Her debut collection, *Patriarchy Blues*, received an American Book Award from the Before Columbus Foundation. Her second collection, *Sublime Subliminal* is available from Floating Bridge Press. Her individual poems and non-fiction pieces are featured at Poets.org, *Poetry Northwest*, *High Country News*, *YES! Magazine*, and elsewhere. She is a National Geographic Explorer (2018-2020) and a Jack Straw Writer (2019). She holds an MFA from Sarah Lawrence College.

Jennifer Richter *(Over Oregon the Flight Attendant Asks If I'm Interested in Water)* is the author of the poetry collections *Threshold* (2010) and *No Acute Distress* (2016), both Crab Orchard Series Selections and Oregon Book Award Finalists. Her work has appeared in many national publications, including *ZYZZYVA*, *Prairie Schooner*, *Poetry*, *Ploughshares*, *The Missouri Review*, *CALYX*, *Poetry Northwest*, and *A Fierce Brightness: Twenty-five Years of Women's Poetry*. She currently teaches in Oregon State University's MFA program.

Ann Stinson *(Ground at my Feet)* grew up on the Cowlitz Ridge Tree Farm near Toledo, Washington. She holds a BA in English from Western Washington University and an MA in East Asian Studies from Columbia University. She splits her time between Portland, where she lives with her husband, and Toledo, where she works on the tree farm. Her first book, *The Ground at My Feet: Sustaining a Family and a Forest*, will be published by Oregon State University Press in Fall 2021.

Rhienna Renée Guedry *(Neighborhood Profiles)* is a writer and artist who found her way to the Pacific Northwest. Her work has been featured in *Empty Mirror*, *HAD*, *Gigantic Sequins*, *Bitch Magazine*, and elsewhere.

Tim Greenup *(Oakdale)* released his first poetry collection, *Without Warning*, with Scablands Books in 2016. His poems have been featured in *LEVELER*, *Pontoon Poetry*, *Sixth Finch*, and elsewhere. He also composes synthesizer music and lives with his family in Spokane, Washington.

Sam Robison *(Goslings)* is a poet and orchardist with deep ties to the Olympic Peninsula. A former resident of Port Townsend and Portland, he is currently an MFA candidate at the University of Montana.

Alexander Ortega *(Nubes)* is a Salt Lake City-based fiction writer currently pursuing an MFA in creative writing from Eastern Oregon University. He seeks to explore absurdism, realism, and the interstices therein to fabricate his own dimensions on the page. When he's not writing or reading, he may occasionally be found playing in a punk band in SLC.

Shannon Amidon *(Don't Be The Bear)* has had poetry appear in *Copper Nickel, The Bellingham Review, RATTLE, Willow Springs, Memorious, Dogwood, Poet Lore* and elsewhere. The recipient of a top Dorothy Sargent Rosenberg Prize and a member of the Squaw Valley Community of Writers, Amadon currently lives in the Berkshires in Western Massachusetts with her family.

Joaquin Fernandez *(A Beginner's Guide To That Perfect Beach Body)* has had his work appear in *Okay Donkey, CheapPop,* and *Pidgeonholes,* among others. A recovering filmmaker from South Florida, he now lives in Portland, Oregon. He can be found on Twitter @Joaqertxranger and on his website joaquinfernandezwrites.com.

Ami Patel (she/her) *(When you say watch your mouth)* is a queer, diasporic South Asian poet and Young Adult Fiction writer. Ami's poetry is published in *perhappened, Red Rock Review,* and *They Rise Like a Wave: An Anthology of Asian American Women Poets,* among others. Find her at amipatelwrites. com or @amiagogo on Instagram and Twitter.

Alexis M Smith *(Wormholes)* is the author of the novels *Glaciers* and *Marrow Island,* a winner of a Pacific Northwest Booksellers Association Award and a Lambda Literary Award. Her short fiction and other writings have appeared in *The Portland Monthly, Tarpaulin Sky, Bon Appétit,* and *The Portland Review.* She lives in Spokane, where she works for Spokane Public Radio and teaches creative writing at Eastern Washington University.

Bethan Tyler *(Digital Autobiography)* is a disabled poet and former radio DJ. She lives in Portland, Oregon with her partner and a cat named Suzie (after Leonard Cohen's "Suzanne"). Her poems have previously been published in *The Chattahoochee Review, Fjords Review,* and *Redivider.*

Gwendolyn Morgan *(Blend, clay, coffee)* is a Pacific Northwest poet and artist who serves in interdisciplinary interfaith care in a medical center. She learned the names of birds and inherited horse hair paint brushes and wooden paint boxes from her grandmothers. The Clark County Poet Laureate 2018-2020 in Washington State, her third book of poetry, *Before the Sun Rises,* is a Nautilus Silver Winner in Poetry. As a multiracial family in a multispecies watershed, Gwendolyn and her spouse Judy A. Rose are committed to equity work and inclusion for all.

Moss was founded by **Connor Guy**, a book editor based in New York, and **Alex Davis-Lawrence**, a filmmaker based in Los Angeles. Both were born and raised in Seattle.

Moss is represented for film/TV by **Alexandra Kordas** at 42 Management & Productions.

Moss.

A journal of the Pacific Northwest.

Editors
Connor Guy
Alex Davis-Lawrence

Managing Editor
Alayna Becker

Contributing Editors
Sharma Shields
Michael Chin
M. Allen Cunningham
Diana Xin
Steven L. Moore

Poetry Editors
Dujie Tahat
Ashley Toliver
Jalayna Carter

Creative Director
Alex Davis-Lawrence

Director of Outreach
Amy Wilson

Programming Coordinator
Cali Kopczick

Grants Manager
Bethany Hays

Additional Design
Ilana Davis-Lawrence

Readers
Angelica Lai
Sasheem Silkiss-Hero
Paisley Green
Kimm Stammen
Elissa Favero
Jamie Bail

Acknowledgments.

Moss is proud to be a subscriber-supported journal. We owe an ongoing debt of gratitude to all our readers, writers, and subscribers—particularly our Patrons, whose exceptional annual support makes our work possible:

Diann Barry and Mark Guy • Thomas and Elizabeth Beck

Max Boyd • Aaron Brown • Alba Conte

Diane Davis • Susan Davis • Ilana Davis-Lawrence

Ronnie-Gail Emden • Joe Grube • Naomi Gibbs

Kris Hattori and Melanie Lim • Paul Lawrence and Cynthia Jones

Sarah Lawrence • Kimberly Roque and Michael Chan

Ann Stinson • Anna and David Straka • Amanda Wong

Aria Woods • Kaye and Robert Woods

Interested in subscribing?

*Visit **mosslit.com** to support Northwest writing*
and get the annual print edition delivered to your door.